Beyond the Sword Maiden

"**An instructive, fascinating account** of the heroine in folk tradition. *Beyond the Sword Maiden* is a valuable resource of exempla for writers, tale tellers and counselors. The relationship of heroism to events in the modern world is particularly meaningful."
　　—**Gilbert Cross**, co-author of *World Folktales*

"**All too often** both traditional storytellers and the media regard the Hero's Journey as the "one true recipe for a good story." In this well-researched and clearly written book, Dorothy Cleveland and Barbara Schutzgruber prove that there are other kinds of stories that are just as essential to the human experience: tales of survival and transformation that we may encounter at any point in our lives. With deep knowledge and personal honesty, these two incredible women bring us the Heroine's Journey, tracing its origins and possibilities from the oldest folktales to life in the 21st century. This book is a much-needed addition to any storyteller's resource library."
　　—**Csenge Virág Zalka**, storyteller, author of *Tales of Superhuman Powers* and *Dancing on Blades*

Beyond the Sword Maiden

A Storyteller's Introduction to the Heroine's Journey

Dorothy Cleveland & Barbara Schutzgruber

Illustrated by Andrea Gruber

Parkhurst Brothers Publishers
MARION, MICHIGAN

www.parkhurstbrothers.com

Parkhurst Brothers books are distributed to the trade through the Chicago Distribution Center,
and may be ordered through Ingram Book Company, Baker & Taylor, Follett Library Resources
and other book industry wholesalers. To order from Chicago Distribution Center, phone 1-800-
621-2736 or fax to 800-621-8476. Copies of this and other Parkhurst Brothers Publishers titles
are available to organizations and corporations for purchase in quantity by contacting Special
Sales Department at our home office location, listed on our website. Manuscript submission
guidelines are available at our website.

Printed in the United States of America
First Edition, 2018
2018 2019 2020 10 9 8 7 6 5 4 3 2 1

ISBN Hardback 978-1-62491-107-1
ISBN: Trade Paperback 978-1-62491-108-8
ISBN: e-book 978-1-62491-109-5

Parkhurst Brothers Publishers believes that the free and open exchange of ideas is essential
for the maintenance of our freedoms. We support the First Amendment of the United States
Constitution and encourage all citizens to study all sides of public policy questions, making up
their own minds. Closed minds cost a society dearly.

Cover and interior design by   Linda D. Parkhurst, Ph.D.
Proofread by   Bill and Barbara Paddack
Acquired for Parkhurst Brothers Inc., Publishers by   Ted Parkhurst

042018

Dedicated to

Heroines

past, present, and future

ACKNOWLEDGEMENTS

The authors gratefully acknowledge
Barbara Frates Buckley, Kathleen Sullivan
and Megan Wells for their editing.

Mary Ellen Schutz of Gentle Editing®, LLC for
her guidance and expertise.

Csenge Virág Zalka for her translations.

Andrea Gruber for her illustrations.

TABLE OF CONTENTS

Introduction ❧ 9

Glossary of Terms ❧ 13

CHAPTER 1
The Importance of Story ❧ 17

CHAPTER 2
Exploring the Sword Maiden's Journey ❧ 23
"Boots and the Troll" ❧ 27
"Mol and the Giant" ❧ 35

CHAPTER 3
Exploring the Heroine's Journey ❧ 52
All Was the Way It Should Be" ❧ 58
"Penta the Handless" ❧ 64

CHAPTER 4
The Importance of the Heroine's Journey ❧ 75

CHAPTER 5
Applications for the Heroine's Journey ❧ 82
Story Development ❧ 84
Psychological Therapy ❧ 86
"Circle of Tears" ❧ 86
Business ❧ 89
"Moving On" ❧ 89

CHAPTER 6

The Hybrid Models ✒ 95

"Call To Arms" ✒ 96

"Handless Maiden" ✒ 104

"Acme Tattoo Parlor" ✒ 108

"Across the Tracks" ✒ 115

CHAPTER 7

Celebration and Sending Forth ✒ 123

Bibliography and Reading List ✒ 127

Reader Extras ✒ 136

Questions and Answers with Authors ✒ 137

Biographies of Authors ✒ 141

Synopsis ✒ 142

INTRODUCTION

As long-time friends and colleagues, we came to writing this book from a common love of story. As storytellers, we mine the nuances of traditional folktales and witness the evolution of personal tales with joy, laughter, and even a few tears. Here are our individual stories, perspectives, and goals for the book.

Dorothy's Perspective

I led a dual life: my professional career in managing a law firm, and my personal life as wife and mother. At age 48, I wanted a healthier balance between these two paths and yet, I was unsure of how to achieve it or even how to imagine what it might look like. I entered a master's program about women in leadership at the University of Minnesota. As part of a paper for a class, I asked colleagues to name their favorite leaders. Not one of them named a woman and, upon further examination, each found it difficult to name any women leaders. Recognizing that my own business background included mainly male mentors and male-oriented achievements (acquisitions, goals, success based on income, winning instead of compromise), I began exploring leadership qualities from a woman's perspective and creating stories about adventurous women.

I was drawn to author, Maureen Murdock, whose book, *The Heroine's Journey*, was a significant resource of how a woman successfully travels the circle of life. Two things happened: 1) I came to see leadership as both an internal and external process, i.e. the Hero's Journey and the Heroine's Journey; and 2) I found I needed to make an internal transformation before tackling the external journey of leading others. Thus, the continued research of the Heroine's Journey.

Stories came to me like a private viewing of a new movie including a big screen with a thunderous sound system. Inundated with sensory data, I needed a structure to frame these stories. The Hero's and Heroine's Journeys work well for me to keep the storyline on its through path to make sense of the story.

Barbara's Perspective

As a child, I was never very good at discerning social subtleties and nuances, but I grew up hearing and reading folktales. I loved those stories. The old folktales of adventure and the least-likely-character-to-succeed winning the day resonated with me. Here I found examples of how characters interacted in a wide range of situations. It was through these stories that I learned how to make sense of the people and the social dynamics around me. In college, I studied comparative folklore as part of both my undergraduate and graduate work. Finding variants of the same storyline across cultural and geographic boundaries reinforced my belief that regardless of external differences, people were not so different deep down.

In 1987, I began working as a freelance performer using traditional material. I found that these stories provided a structure that could be used in creating and telling original stories. The hero adventures were typical fare with most focusing on acquisition and conquest. This structure did not reflect the lives of many of the people around me. Where were the stories of resilience, adaptation, and spontaneity—the stories where plans must change in midstream whenever life presents obstacles? I knew the framework of the Hero's Journey was only the tip of the iceberg in people's real life stories. The stories of survival and emotional triumph did not fit easily into the structure of the hero's tale.

In an airplane, high above the Atlantic, I finally had the chance to read Dorothy's newly completed thesis, "Beyond the Sword Maiden: A Woman's Journey to Leadership through Story." Here was the format I had been looking for—a framework for a personal story that was not the hero's tale. The concept of the Heroine's Journey not only gave a name to the process, it provided a structure that I could use to create original stories for performance.

HOW WE GOT HERE

We began our journey writing this book by generating ideas for a workshop describing the Heroine's Journey. We read, researched and picked each other's brain as to how this journey unfolds in traditional stories. Once we had loosely developed steps for the Heroine's Journey, we travelled across the country presenting and revising the workshop. We acknowledge appreciation to the workshop participants as we learned as much from them as we offered.

This book is a culmination of experience, research, trial, and error. It is a book focused on both the Hero's and Heroine's Journeys to assist writers, storytellers, therapists and counselors in voicing the stories of strong women using the structure of the ever-evolving traditional tale.

Dorothy Cleveland & Barbara Schutzgruber

Glossary of Terms

The following terms are defined as used within the context of this book.

AT INDEX / ATU INDEX / TALE TYPE INDEX

Aarne-Thompson (AT) classification systems are indices used to classify, organize and analyze folklore narratives. Included are the Motif-Index and Tale Type Index. Antti Aarne developed the initial version in 1910; Stith Thompson revised it in 1961. Hans-Jorg Uther revised the classification system in 2004, resulting in the Aarne-Thompson-Uther version. The latest version catalogues some 2,500 basic plots from which European and Near Eastern storytellers have built their tales.

HERO

A hero is male or female (also see Sword Maiden) with masculine energies. The hero's adventure is primarily external with most of the story occurring in the public world. That is, the hero saves an individual and/or community from disaster. The hero also brings a boon back to the community. There is an emotional transformation, but it is not the focus of the story.

HEROINE

A heroine is male or female with feminine energies. The heroine's adventure is primarily internal as the transformation occurs psychologically. However, during the process of the emotional transformation, the heroine may succeed in external events like that of the hero. The story may have other characters, but the focus is on the heroine and her internal struggles with maturing to adulthood and emotional wholeness.

MASCULINE / FEMININE ENERGIES

For the purposes of this book, the terms masculine and feminine identify Jungian archetypal energies in all of us; they are not gender specific. Masculine is the cunning, analytical and physical strength of a person, while feminine is the nurturing, mediating and soulful strength of a person. In addition to these attributes, each behavior has its own way of coming to be. Carol Pearson, author of *Awakening the Heroes Within* and thought leader on archetypal narrative intelligence and transformational leadership, writes:

> The typical "masculine" stance is to find identity
> and truth through separation; the "feminine" stance
> is to find it through identification and connection.
> Although both men and women have access to
> both the "masculine" and "feminine" within,
> the "masculine energies" tend to predominate in
> men and "feminine energies" in women—at least
> from early years until mid-life, at which time
> androgyny becomes the prevailing issue (260).

We need fully developed masculine and feminine energies to become a mature and emotionally balanced individual. Both the Hero's Journey and the Heroine's Journey include aspects of the masculine and feminine energies. The Hero's Journey, which slants toward the masculine warrior, has become the standard journey story in the Western world. Because of this, the Heroine's Journey, with its feminine emphasis on caregiving, is not as well-known. The result, in story and in society, is a lack of balance between the masculine and feminine energies.

SWORD MAIDEN

A sword maiden is a female who travels the Hero's Journey. She is a strong, independent female who kicks butt and is out in the world having grand adventures. She is the warrior St. Joan of Arc, the comic book/TV Wonder Woman, the fictional comic book/TV warrior Xena, and the adventurous archaeologist Lara Croft of *Tomb Raider*. The sword maiden does everything a male hero does and does it just as well. She has amazing tools: swords, golden lassos, clubs, and guns. She rescues those in distress. She rises above others in strength and cunning and always wins the battle. And like her male hero counterpart, she returns home with booty to be shared by all.

CHAPTER 1

The Importance of Story

> Every culture in the history of this planet has created stories: myths,
> fables, legends, folktales. Not all have developed codified laws. Not all
> have created logical argument. Not all have created written language
> and exposition. All developed and used stories (Haven ix).

HOW WE CAME TO STORY

We all tell stories. It comes naturally to us because our brains
are wired for processing the sensory attributes of storytelling. We use
story to teach, counsel, and entertain individuals and organizations.

DOROTHY'S SLANT ON STORY

I did not have many books as a child and my small-town
librarian did not care for children in the library. Thus, my
exposure to literature was limited. I was fortunate in that I
had radio and television. There was a children's story hour on
the radio, daily fodder for my budding imagination, and there
was television, an experimental medium in the 1950s. These
were my windows to the world. After school, I would turn on
the television to watch *The Lone Ranger, The Adventures of
Superman,* and *The Adventures of Robin Hood.*[1] These were
the heroes of my youth. Their lives were filled with adventure
and conflict, making the world a better place to live. Following

---

1. TV syndicated serials of the 1950s starring Clayton Moore, George Reeves,
   and Richard Greene respectively.

the examples of the heroes, I too, lived in an imaginary world of adventure and wonder.

This fantasy life served me well until I entered first grade, when structure and logic were imposed upon my free-thinking soul. I attended Catholic school, where many lessons were taught using bible stories, which often follow the Hero's Journey. At the time, no one knew I had learning disabilities and the Hero's Journey became a familiar and helpful structure for straight narrative, which I used to interpret subjects throughout my school career. Essentially, I would translate abstract thought into story form to understand its meaning.

Barbara's Slant on Story

I grew up listening to stories. Some of my earliest memories are of Nancy Hawkins, an only child teenager who lived next door, reading folktales to me and my brothers and sisters during the summer, under the trees or on her front porch. I, too, attended Catholic school where my teachers, Dominican Sisters, spent the last fifteen minutes of the day reading aloud chapters from historical fiction or classic literature. These books were filled with language far above the reading level of the class, but were stories that caught the imagination. At home, I listened to stories on LP records read by actors and radio personalities, and I would sit at the edge of the adults at family gatherings as they shared stories of adventures and misadventures, ghost stories, and family history. Listening to these stories, I was drawn into the different worlds and introduced to different people. I learned about my ancestors, and began to see patterns and similarities within the storylines.

My fascination with story, especially traditional tales, continued at Eastern Michigan University. There I was introduced to the formal study of folklore, the classification systems used to study variants, and the performance aspect of storytelling through courses in English Literature, Children's Literature, and Applied Drama and Theater for the Young Programs. Here my early perceptions were confirmed—that human beings all tell stories and there are experiences that we all share no matter where we live. Yet we are also wonderfully unique in the way we tell those stories.

OTHER USES OF STORY

Refining our storytelling skills through courses and workshops helped with our artistry, but also included other uses of story. For example, story provides a safe environment to teach social skills. When teaching children about boundaries, which statement has more impact?

1. Don't go into the swamp.
2. Jenny Greenteeth lives in the swamp. If you go into the swamp, she will reach out of the water with slimy, boney arms and pull you under the water.

Children who chose statement #1, more than likely have the social experience to understand the reasoning behind that statement (it is dangerous to enter the swamp) and do not enter the swamp. Many young children, however, do not have the social tools or experience to understand the implications. Statement #2, therefore, is the one that will make sense to them—the swamp is a dangerous place because of Jenny Greenteeth, and we are going to stay out of it. Story in this instance, can help a person learn by presenting an example without risk to the individual. The story provides sensory data which young minds need to understand abstract concepts. This also works with adults as author Annette Simmons writes in *A Safe Place for Dangerous Truths*:

… a well-told story has the power to permeate the mind, body, and emotion of a listener. It can sneak past resistance, engage the right brain's powers of imagination, and anchor an abstract point to any of a thousand connections including past experiences as well as visual, auditory, and even, through imagination, kinesthetic and olfactory sensory reference points (170).

Whether using a cautionary tale to keep a child safe or a metaphorical story of change in a business setting, story presents the possibility for transformation that is acknowledged and internalized once the story is spoken. Stories can help individuals recognize and accept parallel conditions in real life, thus facilitating change in the individual and/or organization. As in our example, we heard and internalized Statement #2 and, therefore, modified our behavior to avoid danger by not entering the swamp.

Story also allows us to make sense of the unknown as in the following examples:

- Early humans trying to make sense of the sun and moon.
- A child trying to comprehend death.
- The chaos caused by mental illness.
- An employee trying to succeed during mergers and downsizing.

For adults, it is sometimes easy to name the steps, analyze the issues and draw conclusions. However, when we are in the thick of trauma or the unknown, it is frequently hard to use words to explain what we want and need. This is where story comes into play. Child psychologists will use story and story play to help children. Politicians, religious leaders, management, and even marketing executives use story to make sense of what is happening in our chaotic world. In the telling of these stories, the truth of the situation is revealed, and enlightenment occurs. Author Clyde W. Ford confirms in his book *The Hero with an African Face*: "When trauma confronts us, individually or collectively, myths are a way of reestablishing harmony in the wake of chaos" (viii-ix).

CHAPTER 2

Exploring the Sword Maiden's Journey

> A hero ventures forth from the world of common
> day into a region of supernatural wonder;
> fabulous forces are there encountered and a decisive victory is
> won: the hero comes back from this mysterious adventure with
> the power to bestow boons on his fellow man (Campbell 30).

THE SWORD MAIDEN'S JOURNEY IS COMMONPLACE, but it is often identified by its masculine title of the "Hero's Journey." The Hero's Journey appears across the globe throughout religion, literature, theater, cinema, and song. American comparative mythology scholar, Joseph Campbell (1904-1987), saw patterns and motifs[2] repeated when studying the myths and folklore from around the world. In 1949, he published his groundbreaking work, *The Hero with a Thousand Faces,* combining his observations with the theories of Freud, Jung, Schopenhauer, and Nietzsche. Campbell herein presented the idea of the *Monomyth,* that all mythic narratives are variations of a single story, and he outlined the Hero's Journey. The Hero's Journey parallels the Sword Maiden's Journey and both include the following basic steps:

1. Call to Adventure
2. Threshold Crossing into the Unknown
3. Tests & Helpers
4. Triumph
5. Return

___
2. A classification of narrative elements found in folktales.

Let us expand this structure with a few details.

Sword Maiden Step 1: Call to Adventure

Early in the story, the sword maiden sets forth from the common world, job, hut or castle. The setting forth can be voluntary—an opportunity to seek one's fortune and have a better life, an assigned task, quest, or even a simple invitation. It can be involuntary—fleeing from danger, abandonment, natural disaster, or abduction—and is not seen as negative victimization. Additionally, it can be whim, curiosity, or even a mistake that sets the sword maiden down a path into the unknown. Sometimes it takes several "calls" before the sword maiden answers. Regardless of how or why the sword maiden sets forth, she is motivated by a sense of destiny; the sword maiden must follow the call, just as we all must "leave home" at some point in our lives.

If the sword maiden refuses to answer the call, she faces negative consequences. The story of Jonah from the Judeo-Christian tradition is one example of what happens if one refuses the call. (God called to Jonah and told him to go to the city of Nineveh. However, Jonah ran away, was thrown into the sea, then swallowed by a large fish. He stayed in the belly of the fish for three days. When Jonah finally decided to obey God's call, the fish expelled Jonah, who finally went to Nineveh as God had commanded.) Perhaps the worst consequences of refusing the call are that the main character is reduced to insignificance, banished to obscurity, and forgotten—for there is no story to tell.

**Sword Maiden Step 2: Threshold:
Crossing into the Unknown**

Now the sword maiden faces the unfamiliar. Often, she crosses the threshold into a world that is completely different from the one she knows. In many stories, she must cross a physical boundary, i.e. "stepping over the line." Traveling into the forest or the mountains, crossing the sea, falling down a rabbit hole or stepping through a looking glass, the sword maiden leaves the safety and security of the known world behind. She must pay or defeat the "guardian" of this new world to enter and continue her adventure. This guardian may be a force that must be physically defeated—or at least outwitted—or a more benevolent creature to whom the sword maiden must prove her worthiness by correctly answering a riddle.

SWORD MAIDEN STEP 3: TESTS & HELPERS

Beyond the threshold, the sword maiden journeys through a world of unfamiliar, yet strangely intimate, forces where she meets odd magical helpers. The helpers may be servants or family members of those she meets in this unfamiliar world or may be some sort of animal, bird, fish, or reptile who takes pity on the sword maiden. Often the helper is a ragged old man or woman to whom the sword maiden has shown compassion and kindness, and who, in return, provides alliances, knowledge, and information. This information may sound like nonsense at the time, but is necessary to complete a future required task. The magical helper often gives tokens to the sword maiden—perhaps everyday items with magical properties, such as a cloak or hat of invisibility; a magical weapon; some sort of food; a tool; or a blessing that brings endless luck or ability. Whatever the token is, the sword maiden needs it to successfully pass the tests and overcome the trials that are placed in her path.

SWORD MAIDEN STEP 4: TRIUMPH

Once the barrier is overcome, the test passed and the monster slain, the sword maiden is identified as superior. She might receive some sort of formal recognition; she might marry; she may come to a new realization of herself; perhaps she is transformed; and/or she may even be granted supernatural power of prophecy. The story may end here, or, it may be merely the end of the first part of her journey. At this point, stories often reflect cultural patterns as the sword maiden faces further obstacles, more tests to be completed. (The number of obstacles is usually determined by the importance of certain numbers within a culture such as 3, 4, 7, 12.) Each additional obstacle requires that the sword maiden cross the threshold, complete another test, and return with the prize until—finally—she faces a supreme ordeal. The stakes are high. Lack of success means death for the sword maiden.

SWORD MAIDEN STEP 5: RETURN

With the final ordeal favorably completed, the sword maiden wins an ultimate reward. Once the final quest has been accomplished successfully, the Sword Maiden must return to the common world. Just as refusing the call in the beginning has negative consequences, refusing to re-enter the common world also has negative consequences. If she stays behind in the alien world, the sword maiden will remain emotionally stunted and is never completely accepted within that community.

Upon her return to the human world, she is required to share her newfound knowledge and/or the physical prize with the community who sent her on her quest. The return trip may be short and easy or it can take years, and be filled with more tests and challenges as in *The Odyssey* by Homer. Regardless, once the sword maiden crosses the return threshold, the transcendental powers she possessed in the alien world must remain behind; she re-emerges with the boon that restores the world.

To illustrate these five steps of the Sword Maiden's Journey, we have chosen two variants of Tale Type ATU 328 Treasures of the Giant (aka Jack and the Beanstalk).[3] Story #1 is Barbara's retelling of a Norwegian folktale from the 1859 collection *Popular Tales from the Norse* by George Webbe Dasent that features a male hero.

STORY #1: "BOOTS AND THE TROLL" © 2017 BARBARA SCHUTZGRUBER

Once upon a time, there was a poor man who had three sons. When he died, the two oldest set out into the world to try their luck, but they refused to take the youngest, Boots, with them.

"As for you, Boots," they said, "you're fit for nothing but to sit and poke about in the ashes."

The older brothers made their way to the palace where one found work with the coachman and the other with the gardener. Boots set out too, taking with him a great kneading-trough.[4] It was the only thing their father had left them, and even though it was heavy to carry, he did not want to leave it behind. He trudged along and finally he, too, came to a palace and asked for work. They told him there was nothing for him, but he smiled so sweetly and begged so nicely that he got a job in the kitchen, bringing in wood and water for the kitchen maid. Boots was quick at his jobs and pleasant to be around, and in no time at all, everyone liked him. His two brothers, on the other hand, were dull and slow, so they got

---

3. ATU Tale Type see Glossary of Terms.
4. A shallow bowl-shaped vessel made of wood, earthenware or bronze. In it, flour and water are mixed and worked into dough.

more kicks than praise, and soon grew envious of Boots.

Just opposite the palace and across the lake, lived a Troll who had seven silver ducks. The ducks could be seen from the palace as they swam on the lake, and the King desperately wanted them.

The two older brothers told the coachman, "Our brother has said he could easily get the King those seven silver ducks, if only he chose to do so."

Well it wasn't long before the coachman told this to the King.

The King called for Boots and said, "Your brothers say you can get me the silver ducks. Go and fetch them."

"I'm sure I never thought nor said anything like that," said Boots.

"You did say so, and you will fetch them," said the King firmly.

"Well!" said the lad. "If I must, I must. Give me a bushel of rye and a bushel wheat and I'll see what I can do."

So, Boots put the rye and the wheat into the kneading-trough he had brought from home. He climbed in and rowed across the lake. When he reached the other side, he began to walk along the shore, sprinkling and tossing the grain. The ducks came scrambling to eat the grain and Boots coaxed them into his kneading-trough. Then he rowed back as fast as he could.

When he was halfway across the lake, the Troll came out of his cave in the face of the rock and saw him.

"HALLOA!" roared the Troll; "Are you the one who carried off my seven silver ducks?"

"AYE! AYE!" said the lad.

"Will you be coming back?" asked the Troll.

"Very likely," said the lad.

Boots gave the seven silver ducks to the King who was pleased to say, "Well done!" And Boots was more liked than ever.

This made his brothers more spiteful and envious. They told the coachman, "Our brother has said he's brave enough to get the King the Troll's bed-quilt, the one with gold patches and silver thread and silver patches with gold thread, if only he chose to do so." Again, the coachman was quick in telling this to the King.

"Well," said the King to Boots. "Your brothers say you're good to steal the Troll's bed-quilt, the one with gold patches and silver thread and silver patches with gold thread."

"I'm sure I never thought nor said anything of the kind," said the lad.

"You did say so, so now you must go and do it or you will lose your life!"

"Well!" said the lad. "If I must, I must. Give me three days to think over the matter."

When the three days were up, Boots rowed across the lake in his kneading-trough and hid near the cave. At last he saw the Troll's daughter come from the cave and hang the quilt out to air. As soon as she had gone back inside, Boots pulled the quilt down and rowed back with it as fast as he could.

When he was halfway across the lake, out came the Troll and

roared, "HALLOA! Are you the one who took my seven silver ducks?"

"AYE! AYE!" said the lad.

"And now, have you taken my bed-quilt with the gold patches and silver thread and silver patches with gold thread?"

"AYE! AYE!" said the lad.

"Will you be coming back?" asked the Troll.

"Very likely," said the lad.

When Boots returned with the gold and silver patchwork quilt, everyone liked him more than ever, and he was made the King's body-servant.

At this, his two brothers were even more upset, and they plotted their revenge. They went to the coachman and said; "Now our brother claims he is clever enough to get the Troll's gold harp for the King. Whenever the harp is played, all who hear it grow glad, no matter how sad they may be."

The coachman went straight away and told the King, who said to Boots, "You have said you can bring me the Troll's gold harp and you shall do it. If you do it, you shall have the princess and half the kingdom. If you don't, you will lose your life."

"I'm sure I never thought nor said anything of the kind," said the lad, "but if I must, I must. Give me six days to think about it."

After six days, Boots put a ten-penny nail, a birch-pin, and a candle into his pocket, and rowed across the lake in his kneading-trough. He walked back and forth in front of the Troll's cave, looking carefully about, until the Troll came out and saw him.

"HALLOA! Are you the one who took my seven silver ducks?"

"AYE! AYE!" said the lad.

"And are you the one who took my bed-quilt with the gold patches and silver thread and silver patches with gold thread?"

"AYE! AYE!" said the lad.

With that, the Troll took hold of him and dragged him into the cave.

"Daughter," said the Troll, "I've caught the one who stole the seven silver ducks and my bed-quilt with gold and silver patches. Put him into the fattening coop, and when he is fat, we'll kill him and make a feast for our friends."

For eight days, Boots was kept in the fattening coop and was fed the best meat and drink. When the eight days were over, the Troll sent his daughter down to slice his finger to see if he was fat.

"Out with your finger!" she said.

But Boots stuck the ten-penny nail out of the coop for her to cut.

"Is he ready?" asked the Troll.

"Nay! He's as hard as iron," said the Troll's daughter when she got back. "We can't take him yet."

For eight more days Boots was fed with the best meat and

drink. Again, the Troll sent his daughter down to see if he was fat yet.

"Out with your finger!" she said.

This time Boots stuck out his birch-pin.

"Is he ready?" asked the Troll.

"Well, he's a bit better," she said when she got back. "But we can't take him yet. He's as hard as wood to chew."

When yet another eight days had past, the Troll told his daughter to go down and see if he was fat now.

"Out with your little finger," said the Troll's daughter when she reached the coop. This time Boots stuck out the candle.

"Is he ready?" asked the Troll.

"Oh yes! He'll do nicely," she reported back.

"Well then," said the Troll, "I'll set out and ask the guests. While I'm gone, you kill him then roast half and boil half."

When the Troll had been gone a while, his daughter brought out a great long knife.

"Is that what you'll use to kill me?" asked Boots.

"Yes, it is," she said.

"It doesn't look very sharp," said the lad. "Would you like me to sharpen it for you? It will be much easier for you to kill me."

So, she let Boots have the knife, and he began to rub and sharpen it on the whetstone.

"I think it's about right," said Boots, "but we should test it. Your braids are as thick as my wrist. We could use one of those to see how well it cuts."

She agreed, but while he held the braid of hair, Boots pulled back her head, and in one gash, cut off the Troll's daughter's head. He roasted half and boiled half, and served her up ready for the Troll and his guests. Then, he dressed himself in her clothes and sat in the shadows in the corner.

When the Troll came home with his guests, he called his daughter to come and eat.

"No thank you," sighed Boots. "I'm so sad and downcast I'm not hungry at all."

"Well," said the Troll, "if that's all, you know the cure. Take down the harp and play a tune."

"Yes!" said the lad in disguise; "but where is it? I can't find it."

"You know where it is," said the Troll. "You used it last. It's hanging over the door."

Boots did not wait to be told twice. He took down the harp and began playing tunes. As he played, he made his way out of the cave and down to the lake. He shoved off the kneading-trough, jumped into it, and rowed away so quickly that the foam flew all around.

When the Troll noticed his daughter had been gone a long time, he went out to see what ailed her. That's when the Troll saw Boots in the trough, far out in the lake.

"HALLOA! Are you the one who took my seven silver ducks?"

"AYE! AYE!" said the lad.

"And are you the one who took my bed-quilt with the gold and silver patches?"

"AYE! AYE!" said the lad.

"And now you have taken off with my gold harp?" screamed the Troll.

"Aye!" said the lad. "I've got it, sure enough."

"But haven't I eaten you up?"

"Oh no! 'Twas your own daughter you ate," answered Boots.

When the Troll heard that, he became so angry, he burst! Boots then rowed back to the Troll's cave and filled the trough with as many bags of gold and silver as it could carry.

When he came to the palace with the gold harp and the treasure, he got the princess and half the kingdom, just as the King had promised. And as for his brothers, Boots treated them well, for he thought they had only wished his good when they said what they had said.

Story #2 features a female sword maiden. In the Gaelic language of Scotland and the Western Isles, she is called Maol a' Chliobain; in Ireland, Hairy Rouchy; in the United States, she is known as Muncimeg or Mutsmag; and in Joseph Jacobs' 1898 collection of English Fairy Tales, she is Molly Whuppie. Using aspects from all these versions, we have included Barbara's retelling of the tale.

STORY #2: "MOL AND THE GIANT"
© 2014 BARBARA SCHUTZGRUBER

There once was a widow who had three daughters. The older two were soft on the eyes, but the youngest was rough around the edges and always spoke her mind with a sharp tongue. Everyone called her Cross-Tempered Mol.

When the girls were old enough, their mother said to them, "Girls, it is time to go out into the world and seek your fortunes."

She baked three loaves—one for each girl.

She broke each loaf in two and said, "Which half will you take? The smaller half and my blessing or the bigger half and my curse?"

The older girls each said, "The big half!" and took the larger parts.

Mol said, "I'll take the little half."

Hearing this, her mother smiled and handed Mol the small half, plus the other halves with her blessing as well, and off they went.

Now the older girls did not want Mol to come with them and try as they might to lose her, she stayed with them with the help of her mother's blessing. Soon the sky grew dark and the air grew cold. The wind came up and it started to rain. Before long the girls were soaked through and chilled to the bone. It was then they realized that they hadn't a clue where they were or which way to go. And night was coming fast.

Just then, they saw a house off in the distance. As they got closer, the older sisters began to have second thoughts.

"We can't just walk up to that house. Who would be living out here in the middle of nowhere? Mol, YOU go and peek in the window."

And so, she did. Well, what she saw was a woman standing at the fire, stirring a large pot. Bread was baking on the hearth-stones. It all smelled oh so good. Mol boldly knocked on the door.

"We're lost, soaked to the skin and chilled to the bone. May we come in to warm by your fire? Would you give us something to eat and let us sleep in your barn for the night? Then in the morning show us the way to town?"

The woman looked at the three girls. "Oh, you can't stay here! My man's a giant and he eats humans! You girls best be off before he gets home."

But Mol just stood there refusing to go away.

She remained at the door looking cold, wet, and hungry until finally the woman said, "Well, all right. But you can't stay long."

And with that, the girls entered the house. The hot soup and fresh bread drove the chill from the girls and, as they sat near the fire, their clothes began to dry. Just as they were about to leave, the ground shook, the door flew open, and there, standing in the doorway, was the biggest man they had ever seen. He was eight feet tall. His shoulders filled the door-frame. He had muscles upon muscles and carried a massive weapon. This glave[5] had a staff as tall as he was and, on its

5.   A glave is an ancient polearm weapon consisting of a long sharp knife on the end of a pole.

end, a blade the length of Mol's arm, sharp as could be and glowing with light.

"Oh! I see we have company—for—dinner!"

With that the Giant's wife walked right up to him and said, "Now you leave those girls alone. They were lost, wet, and hungry, and they're heading out now. You leave them be! You hear me!"

But the Giant said, "Oh, they can't leave now. It's too dark and cold. The storm is only getting worse. No, they must stay the night."

Now the Giant lived with his mother, his wife and their three red-haired daughters. The girls all sat by the fire talking and laughing. Mol and her sisters looked in awe at the beautiful amber necklaces that the Giant's girls wore. When their mother was not looking, the Giant's daughters gave a nod to their father and grandmother and made necklaces out of knotted straw for Mol and her sisters. The Giant and the old hag sat in the corner—watching and smiling.

When it was time to sleep, all six girls piled into the same bed. When they blew out the light, the room was so dark that Mol could not see her hand in front of her face. The Giant's three girls were quickly asleep. Mol's sisters were asleep not long after. Only Mol lay awake in the darkness.

Something was bothering Mol. Something wasn't quite right, but she didn't know what. She lay there in the dark fingering the knotted straw necklace. It felt so rough and scratchy, not cold and smooth like the amber bead necklaces the Giant's girls wore. And then Mol remembered the girls nodding to their father and grandmother as they sat in the corner—watching—smiling. Quietly, without disturbing the others, Mol took the straw necklaces off herself and her sisters and switched them with the amber necklaces of the Giant's girls.

Now it was just then that a thirst came over the Giant and he called to his ghillie,[6] "Kill one of the human girls and bring me her blood."

"How will I know them from your own girls?"

"There are beads of amber on my daughters' necks and knots of straw on the others."

Just as Mol was starting to drift off, she heard the door open. Someone had entered the room. Mol lay still. She couldn't see a thing, but she knew someone was there. Then she felt the ghillie's hand on her throat. She didn't move; she hardly even breathed. When the ghillie felt the silky-smooth necklace on Mol's neck, he moved on. He moved from girl to girl, passing over the three with amber necklaces. When he touched a rough, scratchy straw necklace, the ghillie killed that girl quick as can be and took her blood to the Giant who drank it down and asked for more to be brought to him. So, the ghillie killed the next girl; the Giant drank and asked for more; and the ghillie killed the third.

No sooner had the ghillie left the room the third time, when Mol woke her sisters and they quietly slipped out the window.

"Thief! Stop, thief!" cried the amber necklaces.

Hearing this, the Giant ran into the room. Seeing that his three daughters were dead, he ran after those girls. Mol and

---

6. A servant who specializes in hunting and fishing.

her sisters ran. And the Giant ran. And Mol and her sisters ran. The Giant was gaining on them. The girls ran, their legs aching, their lungs burning and the Giant getting closer and closer—reaching for them—reaching for them!

Just then, the girls came to a halt at the edge of cliff overlooking a deep gorge and waterfall. They were trapped. Mol plucked a single hair from her head and, with the help of her mother's blessing, it became a bridge—ever so thin. With a screaming sister under each arm, Mol went forward—crossing the Bridge of One Hair.

The Giant stood on his side of the waterfall, too large and too heavy to cross the Bridge of One Hair and yelled, "You got my three daughters killed! Mol, don't you EVER come back here again!"

And Mol just looked back at that Giant and said, "Maybe I will and maybe I won't! I'll come and go as my business brings me!"

And off the girls went as the sun was coming up.

Now Mol and her sisters had escaped from the Giant, but they were still lost. It was then that they heard the distant sound of hunting horns, and over the hill came a group of riders. It was the Queen of that land out for her morning ride with all her court. The Queen looked down at the three girls who were rather shabby in dress and appearance, yet wore beautiful amber necklaces.

When she heard their story, she said, "Mol, you're a smart girl. You're a clever girl. You're a brave girl. You and your sisters may come and live at the palace."

One day the Queen sat beside Mol and said, "Mol, you're a smart girl. You're a clever girl. You're a brave girl. Stories say the Giant has a chest of silver and a chest of gold. Bring me the Giant's treasure and your oldest sister may marry my oldest son."

Now Mol's oldest sister and the Queen's oldest son had fallen in love and they said to her, "Oh, come on Mol. Give it a try."

And Mol said, "All right. I'll try."

Off she went back to the Giant's house. She waited until everyone was gone and entered the house. Where would the chests of silver and gold be kept? She looked in the cupboards. She looked in the drawers. She moved loose stones on the hearth and loose planks on the floor. She looked high and low. At last, she came to the Giant's room. There in the corner were the two chests that held the treasure. Just as Mol was about to take them, the house shook. The Giant was home and under the bed Mol hid. There she stayed waiting. Watching—until at last the Giant fell asleep—right on top of the chests.

When she could tell by his breathing that he was asleep, Mol slipped out and moved a bench next to the sleeping Giant. Then she went to the stream and got cold stones. Slowly, carefully she slipped the cold stones under the sleeping Giant. The Giant shifted in his sleep moving away from the stones. Carefully, Mol moved the stones bit by bit. The Giant slowly shifted off the chests and onto the bench.

When he was clear of the chests, Mol put a chest under each arm.

But as she left the house, the chests cried out, "Thief! Stop, thief!"

With that the Giant was awake and chased after Mol. Mol ran. And the Giant ran. And Mol ran. The chests were heavy, and the Giant was gaining, but Mol kept running—her legs aching, her lungs burning, and the Giant getting closer and closer—reaching out to grab her hair. But she got to the Bridge of One Hair and quickly ran across.

The Giant stood on his side and shouted, "You got my daughters killed and now you've stolen my silver and gold! Mol, don't you EVER come back here again!"

Mol just looked back at that Giant and said, "Maybe I will and maybe I won't! I'll come and go as my business brings me!"

And off she went to give the chests to the Queen and to dance at her sister's wedding.

Time passed. On another day, the Queen sat beside Mol and said, "Mol, you're a smart girl. You're a clever girl. You're a brave girl. Stories say that the Giant has a great weapon that can cut through anything. Bring me the Blade of Light and your second sister can marry my second son."

Now Mol's second sister and the second son of the Queen had fallen in love and they said to her, "Oh, come on Mol. Give it a try."

And Mol said, "All right. I'll try."

Off she went back to the Giant's house. Again, Mol waited until everyone was gone and entered the house. She hid herself up in the rafters and waited. That night as the Giant's wife made the stew, Mol threw handfuls of salt down into the pot.

The salty food caused the Giant such a thirst that he called to his ghillie, "Go out to the stream and bring me water."

"Master, it's a dark night, and the stream is a long way off."

"Then take the Blade—that will light your way."

Hearing this, Mol slipped from the rafters and out of the house. She hid near the stream. When the ghillie set down the glowing Blade to get the water, Mol leapt out, grabbed the Blade of Light and, in one stroke, cut off the ghillie's head.

"Thief! Stop, thief!" cried the Blade as its light flashed over the hills. And the Giant came running after Mol.

Mol ran. And the Giant ran. And Mol ran, but the pole was long and awkward, the blade was heavy, and the Giant was gaining on her. But Mol kept running—her legs aching, her lungs burning, and the Giant getting closer and closer—reaching out to grab her hair. But she got to the Bridge of One Hair and quickly ran across.

The Giant stood on his side and bellowed, "You got my daughters killed, stole my silver and gold, and now you've killed my ghillie and taken the Blade of Light! Mol, don't you EVER come back here again!"

And Mol just looked back at that Giant and said, "Maybe I will and maybe I won't! I'll come and go as my business brings me!"

And off she went to give the Blade of Light to the Queen and to dance at her sister's wedding.

Time passed. The Queen sat beside Mol once more and said, "Mol, you're a smart girl. You're a clever girl. You're a brave girl. Stories say that the Giant has a great Buck Goat with the finest gold bells around its neck. Bring me the Buck Goat and you can marry my youngest son."

Well, Mol looked at the youngest son who said to her, "It's true Mol, you're a smart girl. You're a clever girl. You're a brave girl. And you're a good a sister, too. I'd be lucky to get a wife like you."

And Mol said, "All right. I'll try."

Off she went—back to the Giant's house. When she knew that everyone was asleep, Mol made her way to the pens and found the great Buck Goat. She blocked up the bells with moss, placed a band around the Buck Goat's mouth so he could not cry out, and tried to lead him away. But that Buck Goat reared and kicked until the stuffing fell from the bells. And the sound that came from those bells was loud enough to wake the dead. Mol hoisted that great Buck Goat over her shoulders and began to run, the Giant at her heels.

Mol ran. And the Giant ran. And Mol ran. The Giant was enraged and ran faster and faster. Mol ran and ran. The Giant got closer and closer—reaching out to grab her hair. She could hear Giant right behind her. He was just about to catch her when she got to the Bridge of One Hair and quickly ran across.

The Giant stood on his side and roared, "You got my daughters killed, stole my silver and gold, killed my ghillie, took the Blade of Light, and now you've stolen the great Buck Goat with the golden bells! Mol, don't you EVER come back here again!"

And Mol just looked back at that Giant and said, "Maybe I will and maybe I won't! I'll come and go as my business brings me!"

Off she went to give the great Buck Goat with the golden bells to the Queen and to dance at her own wedding.

It was at the wedding that the Queen came and sat beside Mol and said, "Mol, you're a smart girl. You're a clever girl. You're a brave girl. There is one last task I have for you. Bring me the Giant's brass shield, along with his bow and quiver of arrows, and you shall be queen of the land when I'm gone."

"All right. I'll try," was all Mol said.

And off she went—back to the Giant's house. She waited until everyone was gone and entered the house. She searched high and low looking for the brass shield, the bow and the quiver of arrows. At last she came to the Giant's room. There hanging on the wall at the head of the bed was the shield, the bow and the quiver. Mol was about to take them when the house shook—the Giant was home. And under the bed she slid. Mol lay there until at last the Giant climbed into bed. The mattress sunk low, almost touching her and Mol waited. When she could tell by his breathing that the Giant was asleep, she slipped out from under the bed and slowly, carefully, reached up right over the head of the sleeping Giant. Slowly, carefully she stretched up onto her tiptoes. Stretching, reaching, right over the sleeping Giant, she brought down the bow and quiver. Then she reached up and took hold of the shield, slowly, carefully, lifting it off the hooks—balancing the weight just so. And then it fell to the floor as a huge hand grabbed Mol! The Giant was awake; Mol was caught.

"I've got you now! What shall I do to you after all that you've done to me? I know. I'll cut off your head."

Now Mol was a smart girl, a clever girl, a brave girl, and she could think fast on her feet.

So, she said, "Oh, is that all? I would do worse to you."

"Well, then I'll put you on a rack and roast you alive!"

"Oh, is that all? I would do worse to you."

"And what would that be?" asked the Giant.

"Well, if I were you, I'd put me in a sack and hang that sack from the top of a tree. Then I'd go to the wood, find a great club and beat the sack until I was dead."

"That's a grand idea and exactly what I will do!"

So, the Giant threw Mol into a sack, tied it tight, flung it high into a tree, and leaving his mother to stand watch, set off to find the biggest club he could. Mol waited. When enough time had passed for the Giant to be long gone, Mol began to laugh.

"Have you gone mad? Why are you laughing?" called the old hag.

"Tis pearls and gold and diamonds here."

"What's that?"

"Tis pearls and gold and diamonds here."

"Let me in to see for myself."

"No. You can't come in, for tis pearls and gold and diamonds here."

"You will let me in!"

And with that the old hag untied the sack, pulled Mol out and climbed inside. Mol quickly tied the sack shut, picked up the brass shield, the bow and quiver of arrows and slipped around the side of the house.

Just then the Giant returned and began swinging at the sack.

The old hag howled in pain calling out, "Tis myself in this sack you fool."

"I know it's yourself that's in it, Mol."

It was then the Giant saw Mol slipping off through the trees with the shield, bow, and quiver and he was after her. Mol ran. And the Giant ran. And Mol ran. The Giant ran faster and faster. Mol ran and ran and the Giant got closer and closer. The ground trembled, and Mol fell. The Giant gained ground, but Mol picked up herself and kept running. The Giant was reaching out to grab her hair. She could feel his hot breath on her neck and his fingers brushing against her hair. He was just about to catch her when she got to the Bridge of One Hair and quickly ran across.

The Giant stood on his side and thundered, "You got my daughters killed, stole my silver and gold, killed my ghillie, took the Blade of Light, stole the great Buck Goat with the golden bells, got my mother sorely beaten, and stole my brass shield, my bow and quiver of arrows! Mol, don't you EVER come back here again!"

And Mol just looked back at that Giant and said, "Maybe I will and maybe I won't! I'll come and go as my business brings me!"

With that the Giant became more enraged. He took a great leap across the gorge, but missed his step, falling to the bottom. There he lay dead at the base of the waterfall.

Mol bought the brass shield, the bow and quiver of arrows to the Queen. Mol and the youngest son were made heirs, and when the Queen died, they ruled that land long and well.

Now that we have two stories to connect to the Sword Maiden's Journey, we can review each step of the journey in more detail. **Table 2.1** provides an overview.

Table 2.1 "Boots and the Troll" vs. "Mol and the Giant" Comparison

Sword Maiden	"Boots and the Troll"	"Mol and the Giant"
Step 1: Call to Adventure	The father dies. Boots and his brothers set off to try their luck in the world.	The mother tells Mol and her sisters to seek their fortunes in the world.
Step 2: Threshold Crossing into the Unknown	Boots arrives at the palace.	Mol and her sisters enter the giant's house.
Step 3: Tests & Helpers	Boots carries the heavy kneading-trough and charms his way into being hired.	The giant's wife helps them with food and a dry place to stay. Straw necklaces are a clue that something bad is going to happen. Mol's mother's blessing makes the Bridge of One Hair possible.
Step 4: Triumph	Boots is quick, ready, and well-liked by all at the palace.	Mol saves herself and her sisters from death and they escape across the Bridge of One Hair.
Step 5: Return	Boots is promoted and his status improves.	The three girls are found by the queen and given a safe home.
Repetition of Steps 1-5	The king presents repeated tasks: capture the silver ducks, the bed-quilt with gold and silver patches, and the magic harp. Boots crosses the lake to the troll's cave each time.	The queen presents repeated tasks: capture of the chests of silver and gold, the Blade of Light, the Buck Goat, and the brass shield with bow and arrows. Mol crosses into the giant's land each time.
Step 5: Final Return	After outwitting the troll and killing his daughter, Boots returns with added treasure, marries the princess, is given half the kingdom, and treats his brothers well.	Mol and her husband rule the land long and well.

In comparing these two stories, both Story #1 and Story #2 follow the Hero/Sword Maiden's Journey. Both Boots and Mol receive and accept calls to adventure, cross into unknown territory, pass tests successfully, return triumphant, and go on to repeat the pattern. Not only do they both follow the same journey but many of the motifs found in each story are identical: rejected by older siblings, living in a palace, outwitting the Troll/Giant to steal from them to help a friendly King/Queen, decapitating the daughter/servant, and a scolding match between the Boots/Moll and the Troll/Giant. Mol, the sword maiden, behaves just as Boots, her hero counterpart, does.

CONCLUSION

Odysseus, Beowulf, Jack and the Beanstalk, Bilbo and Frodo Baggins, Luke Skywalker, and more recently Harry Potter, are all examples of male characters in mainstream Western literature and film who follow this journey. We know these heroes; we see them often. Due to cultural and societal restrictions, girls and women have not often been encouraged to "go forth" on the Sword Maiden's Journey. When they do appear in the popular male Hero's Journey, they are often relegated to the role of sidekick or helper for a male main character, (Hermione Granger in *Harry Potter* and Morgiana in *"Ali Baba and the Forty Thieves"*). However, with a little digging into the old tales, we find females embarking on the Sword Maiden's Journey: Atalanta (from Greek Mythology), Gretel (from the Grimm Brothers' "Hansel and Gretel"), Hua Mulan (the historical Chinese warrior), Lady Mary (in the English folktale "Mr. Fox"), and Hiiaka (patron goddess of Hawaii) to name a few.

The adventure, suspense, and excitement of the Sword Maiden's Journey captures the imagination. If we look at the events in the lives of those around us through this lens, we will find count-less stories waiting to be told. Who are the sword maidens who have touched your life—those courageous women and girls who heeded the call, fought the good fight, won glory, and returned to share their bounty and knowledge with others? The Sword Maiden's Journey can be an effective model for shaping stories of life. Every new project can be a call to adventure. Teachers, mentors, and super-visors become the helpers who guide us along the way and offer tools to make the journey easier. We encounter giants and dragons in business conflicts, scheduling delays, and budget cuts. We are always wiser once the project is completed, even if the project fails. We receive acknowledgment and glory for successes and sometimes profit monetarily. The greatest reward is to eventually be known as an elder and to mentor others on their journeys.

The Sword Maiden's Journey is a goal-oriented structure that works particularly well when faced with specific tasks that need to be completed. However, what if the challenges faced are not those based on the achievement of measurable tasks? What about the emotional journeys we take as we mature? Here is where the Heroine's Journey comes into play.

CHAPTER 3

Exploring the Heroine's Journey

> Working as a therapist with women, particularly between the ages of thirty and fifty, I have heard a resounding cry of dissatisfaction with the successes won in the marketplace. This dissatisfaction is described as a sense of sterility, emptiness, and dismemberment, even a sense of betrayal. These women have embraced the stereotypical male heroic journey and have attained academic, artistic, or financial success; yet for many the question remains, "What is all of this for?" (Murdock 1).

THE HEROINE'S JOURNEY IS NOT AS WELL-KNOWN as the Sword Maiden's Journey. Though we may travel this journey at least once in a lifetime, we don't often talk about what we went through. However, the Heroine's Journey is a critical model for maturation and healing. It is the process of balancing the emotional masculine and feminine energies within ourselves when a trauma occurs that disrupts the balance. Through this process, the individual is transformed from a dependent child to an independent adult who is capable of handling adult responsibilities.

In our research, we found several books about the Heroine's Journey; most of the writings focus on healing women who have gone through trauma. Each author listed steps to follow on the Heroine's Journey. **Table 3.1** provides an overview of each book's perspective.

Table 3.1 Books outlining steps for the Heroine's Journey

C. Tang	M. Murdock	C. S. Pearson	E. Davis/ C. Leonard
The Story Sensei: Heroine's Journey Worksheet	*The Heroine's Journey: Woman's Quest for Wholeness*	*The Hero Within: Six Archetypes We Live By*	*The Circle of Life: Thirteen Archetypes for Every Woman*
Home & Separation from the Feminine	Separation from the Feminine	The Hero's Journey	The Daughter
The Awakening	Identifies with the Masculine	From Innocent to Orphan	The Maiden
The Road of Trials	The Road of Trials		The Blood Sister
The Illusory Boon of Success	The Illusory Boon of Success	The Wanderer	The Lover
Death; All is Lost	Strong Women Can Say No		The Mother
Support from Others; Descent to The Goddess	The Initiation and Descent to The Goddess	The Warrior	The Midwife
Epiphany; Reconnect with the Feminine	Urgent Yearning to Reconnect with the Feminine	The Martyr	The Amazon
Rebirth; Healing	Healing the Mother / Daughter Split	The Magician	The Matriarch
Return to the Perfect World	Finding the Inner Man with Heart	The Return	Priestess Sorceress Crone Dark Mother
Integration	Beyond Duality		The Transformer

Table 3.1 (continued) Books outlining steps for the Heroine's Journey

R. A. Johnson	A. B. Chinen	M. E. Harding	V.E. Frankel
She: Understanding Feminine Psychology	*The Waking World: Classic Tales of Women and the Heroic Feminine*	*The Way of All Women*	*From Girl to Goddess: The Heroine's Journey through Myth and Legend*
The Birth of Psyche	Many Versions One Drama	All Things to All Men	Growing Up: The Ordinary World
The Youth of Psyche	The Devil	The Ghostly Lover	
Eros	Amputation and Helplessness		
The Confrontation	Questions and Silence	Work	Journey through the Unconscious
Love or In Love		Friendship	Meeting the Other
The Dismissal of Eros	Rescue	Marriage	
The Suffering of Psyche	Exile and Healing	Maternity	
The Tasks	The Water of Life	Off the Beaten Track	Facing the Self
	The Deep Feminine / Woman's Spirituality and the Body	Autumn and Winter	Goddesshood and Wholeness
A Modern Psyche	Reconciliation	Psychological Relationship	

We developed our Heroine's Journey steps based on the accumulated information from these authors, our workshops on this subject, and the reading of folktales of Tale Type ATU 706 Girl Without Hands. We adapted these steps to assist with writing and telling stories of the Heroine's Journey.

HEROINE'S JOURNEY STEPS
1. Unprotected Innocence
2. Villain appears
3. Trauma Split
4. Departure
5. Wilderness 1/Basic Needs
6. Safety
7. Betrayal
8. Wilderness 2/Recovery
9. Wholeness

HEROINE STEP 1: UNPROTECTED INNOCENCE

The story of the Heroine's Journey always begins with the home situation as idyllic, but rapidly changes when the father's source of income declines, the father and mother die, flee or are absent, which causes the children to be left on their own. In psychology, the feminine energies of nurturing and protection are missing. The heroine is naïve, alone, and subject to physical and/or emotional wounding.

HEROINE STEP 2: VILLAIN APPEARS

The villain is an evil character whose attributes include deceit, murder, destruction of property, and greed. The villain may be male or female and will reappear in the story. The presence of a villain is a clever plot tool employed to push the heroine towards transformation. If the heroine does not change, she is repeatedly tricked until she learns to recognize the villain as evil and not trustworthy.

HEROINE STEP 3: TRAUMA SPLIT

Trauma occurs when the heroine undergoes a physical and/or

emotional wounding at the hands of a male relative or a masculine entity. Trauma is also that part of the plot during which the heroine suffers a harm that destroys her innocence. The heroine must move forward or die; she cannot return to a state of innocence again. The trauma split causes the imbalance of the masculine and feminine energies. The cutting off hands symbolizes the heroine is no longer a part of the family and/or community.

HEROINE STEP 4: DEPARTURE

Her decision to leave home overcomes the heroine's fear of a world outside her immediate family. Her departure causes her to become dependent upon strangers for help. This Step requires courage, curiosity, and the willingness to take personal risks. She begins to develop her masculine behavior when she stands up to her male relative and refuses to stay in a place where she may be further harmed.

HEROINE STEP 5: WILDERNESS 1/BASIC NEEDS

The heroine travels alone through the wilderness—a place filled with natural elements such as trees, plants, animals, magical spirits, water, and earth—where she spends time in self-reflection and learns to survive on her own. She finds food and shelter. She begins to know who she is and what she wants. The wilderness may be metaphorical, but it is always a place of learning self-survival.

HEROINE STEP 6: SAFETY

The heroine is found by a male, usually royalty or a wealthy merchant, who feels sorry for her and wants to take care of her. The heroine believes she is safe in the new environment, but the safety is only temporary. She must learn that she is never safe when another has control of her life. In this Step, the heroine learns that she must not let her life slip away; she must be proactive to insure her survival and happiness. While the heroine is being cared for by others, she is learning and developing social skills, which she previously did not possess.

HEROINE STEP 7: BETRAYAL

The villain from Step 2 reappears and betrays the heroine. However, it appears to her as though an ally, such as a husband or brother, is to blame. Because the heroine now realizes that even kind people are capable of tricking, wounding, and betraying, she must learn to manage her own life. To do so, she must return to isolation as she similarly did in Step 4.

HEROINE STEP 8: WILDERNESS 2/RECOVERY

It is in Step 8 that the Heroine matures or "grows back her hands." The regrowth of hands signifies that the heroine is useful once again. She is fully equipped with what a woman needs to manage the world in which she lives. She is not alone this time in the wilderness; she is helped by a wise person, usually an older woman or a magician. She thoroughly contemplates her past life, accepts that she can never return home, and determines how she wants to live in the future. This is a critical step. If the heroine does not take ownership of her life, she remains dependent on others to make decisions for her, and thus, does not mature into an adult who can handle adult responsibilities. If the heroine fails to mature during this step, she returns to Step 6 to be betrayed once more.

HEROINE STEP 9: BALANCE

Now all the pieces of the heroine's life come together. In many stories, the heroine becomes a queen through marriage and rules with her king in peace for many years. It is a time of maturity when both masculine and feminine energies are balanced. The heroine has matured so that she sees beyond her own life to that of others; she becomes communal; she identifies and connects with humanity. This is not to say that she will not encounter future problems; rather, the balance of the feminine and masculine energies enables her to cope with even the paradoxes of life in which the conflicts cannot be resolved.

To illustrate the Heroine's Journey structure here are two versions of ATU 706 Girl Without Hands. Story #1 is Dorothy's retelling of the folktale using aspects from seven cultural variations.

STORY #1: "ALL WAS THE WAY IT SHOULD BE"
©2016 DOROTHY CLEVELAND

> Once upon a time, there was a miller and his wife. The couple had two children, a boy and a girl. All was the way it should be.
>
> One day, the miller was working in the mill when his foot was crushed by the millstone. The foot became so infected, he soon died from gangrene. His wife became hysterical, ran off into the woods, and was never seen or heard from again.
>
> The Brother, who was older, said to his sister, "You run the house, while I run the mill."
>
> In time, the Brother came of age and took a wife who was as beautiful as she was evil. The Brother's new wife was jealous of her sister-in-law's power and authority. One day while the Brother was working at the mill, his wife broke all the furniture in the house.
>
> When he came home, his wife groaned, "Look what your sister has done!"

"We can get new furniture," said the Brother calmly.

The Sister remained silent.

A couple of weeks later, while the Brother was away in the city, his wife cut off the head of the mule that pulled the millstone.

When the Brother returned, his wife lamented, "Look at what your sister has done!"

The Brother replied, "The mule was old anyway. I will get a new mule."

The Sister remained silent.

Then the Brother went on a long journey across the sea. He told his sister to be kind and gentle with his wife, for she was with child. The Sister promised she would. When his wife gave birth, she cut off her newborn's head.

When the Brother came home, his wife wailed, "Look at what your sister has done!"

The Brother looked upon the blood-soaked crib and went into a rage.

"You shall suffer for what you have done," thundered the Brother, and grabbing his sister by the hair, he dragged her to the mill.

There the Brother cut off both of her hands. The Sister remained silent.

The Sister, knowing that she was no longer safe, broke away from her brother's grasp and ran alone into the woods. There she rolled her stumps in dried moss and mud until they stopped bleeding. As her stumps healed, the Sister lived on the fruits and roots of the woods that she could gather with her mouth; she lapped water like an animal. She slept in hollow trees and covered herself with leaves under the starlit sky.

One day, the Sister came upon an apple orchard. She rushed forward to partake of the fruit. The trees bent their branches low so she could grasp the fruit with her mouth. This orchard belonged to the King who happened to be walking through it and saw a young maiden eating his fruit.

Seeing that the Sister was so thin and gray, the King asked, "Are you real or are you a ghost?"

"I am real," she said.

The King fell in love with the Sister at that moment and took her as his wife. He commanded the best silversmith in the kingdom to fashion a pair of silver hands for his new bride and she wore the silver hands proudly. All was the way it should be.

Soon the King went to war and asked his mother to watch over his wife as she was with child. The King said he wanted to be notified as soon as the baby was born. When her time came, the Sister, now Queen, gave birth to a fine baby boy. The King's mother sent a messenger with the announcement to the King. The messenger stopped at the mill of the Brother and his wife and asked for water and rest. The messenger told the Brother's wife that the "Queen with No Hands" had a baby and he was carrying the announcement to the King. The Brother's wife was furious that her sister-in-law was now a queen. While the messenger slept, the Brother's wife wrote a new message and exchanged it for the original one.

The King read the new message, "Your wife has given birth to a changeling. What shall I do?"

He wrote a return message instructing his mother, "Take care of them both until I return."

The messenger stopped at the mill on his way back to the King's mother. Once again, as the messenger slept, the Brother's wife substituted a different message. When the King's mother read the message, she was aghast.

The message was boldly written, "Kill both and keep the hearts as proof."

The King's mother, having become fond of her son's wife, ordered a woodsman to kill a doe and its fawn and bring the hearts to her, which she placed in a gold box for safe keeping.

She showed the message to her daughter-in-law saying, "You and the baby must leave at once."

The King's mother bound the baby to the Queen's breast and sent them forth. The Queen and her baby wandered through the woods all night. At daybreak, they arrived exhausted at a small cottage. Written above the door were the words "Here All Dwell Free." Using her silver hands, she knocked on the door.

An old woman answered, "Welcome, dear Queen. I have been waiting for you."

"How did you know I was the Queen?"

"Oh," said the old woman, "The woods know all that is happening in this corner of the world."

The Queen entered the cottage and stayed there, while raising her child. Without servants, she fumbled with her silver hands as she cared for the baby. But soon, the Queen simply put the silver hands into a drawer and went about her daily chores using only her stumps. As the days went by, the Queen wondered about her missing hands. At night, she would wave her handless arms into the stream of moonlight that entered her room and, while in the moonlight, the shadow of her former hands appeared. But when the sun rose, the hands were missing again.

One morning the old woman smiled, "I see a bit of moonlight has entered the day."

The Queen looked at her stumps and saw the buds of fingers emerging.

"Oh," rejoiced the Queen, "Can it be true? Is it possible for me to grow back my hands?"

The old woman nodded, "With patience and hard work, all things are possible."

Day by day, week by week, the Queen measured her new fingers, and like her young son's hands, they grew. Both mother and son learned to use tools, pick berries, and plant flowers. All was the way it should be.

When the King returned from war, he asked to see his wife and baby. His mother showed him the message she received, and from the gold box she brought forth the two hearts.

The King said, "That is not the message I wrote."

It was then the King's mother informed him that the Queen and baby were sent into the woods.

For seven years, the King roamed the kingdom searching for the Queen and their child. His beard grew long and his royal clothing became dirty and torn. Finally, he arrived weary at a small cottage. Written above the door were the words "Here All Dwell Free" and he asked for a place to rest. The old woman let him sleep upon a cot. She told the Queen that her husband was in the next room. The Queen was alarmed for she had feared the King would kill her and their son if he ever found them. However, she knew she must confront him because she was no longer willing to live in fear of being hunted down.

The Queen woke the King with a touch of her hand. The King did not recognize her until she brought forth from the drawer the silver hands he had made for her so long ago. Words of truth poured forth. The Queen told the King of her sister-in-law's lies.

Then the old woman said in a soft, clear voice, "It was the miller's wife who meddled with the messages to and from the King."

"Come," the Queen said to their son. "Come and meet your father."

With joy and happiness, the three embraced and ate their fill for they were hungry.

"Now," the King said soberly, "we must deal with the miller's wife. Your brother must not be held by this lie any longer."

The King and Queen with their child traveled to the mill. There they told the truth to the Brother. He immediately ordered his strongest horse to be brought to him. Grabbing his wife by her hair, he tied her braid to the horse and sent it galloping across the field. When horse returned, all that remained was the braid.

The King invited the Brother to join them in the castle, which he did. The King and Queen renewed their marriage vows and ruled in peace and harmony for the rest of their days. All was the way it should be.

The second example, Story #2, is a summary of "Penta the Handless" from *IL PENTAMERONE: or The Tale of Tales* by Giovanni Batiste Basile and translated by Sir Richard Burton, K.C. M.G., 1893.

STORY #2: "PENTA THE HANDLESS"
© 2016 DOROTHY CLEVELAND

The King of Preta-secca did not have a wife and so he decided to take his sister, Penta, as his bride. Penta was greatly offended and told the King that she would not participate in such a partnership and shut herself away for a month. During that time, Penta began to wonder what it was that attracted her brother to herself for she was not considered the most beautiful of maidens. She sent the request to her brother who responded that it was her hands that he desired. Penta then called her servant and demanded the servant cut off her hands. The servant did so with as little pain as possible for Penta. Penta sent her two lifeless hands on a silver plate to her brother.

Her brother was furious and had Penta sealed into a barrel and tossed into the sea. Penta floated and tossed among the waves finally arriving upon the shore. The chief of the sailors, Masiello, opened the barrel and brought Penta to his wife for care. As soon as Masiello was gone, the jealous wife put Penta back into the barrel and tossed it out to sea again.

The King of Terra-Verde was sailing and found the barrel at sea. He had his sailors retrieve the barrel and once opened, the King took Penta to his kingdom and made her the hand-maiden for his Queen. The Queen died without producing an heir and her dying wish was for the King to marry Penta, which the King did. Nine months later, Penta produced a male heir for her King. A message was sent to the King who was away during the happy event. However, the courier was waylaid by Masiello's wife who changed the happy message to say that the King's wife had given birth to a dog. Unaware of the exchange of message, the courier took the response from the King who sent a reply to take care of Penta and the child until he returned. Again, waylaid by Masiello's wife, the message was exchanged so that when the courier arrived at the palace, the message read that Penta and the child were to be burned. Instead, the councilors expelled Penta and the child from the kingdom.

Penta, the child bound to her breast, travelled to Lago-truvolo where a great magician lived. The Magician wept at Penta's story and claimed her as his daughter providing housing for her and child in his palace. Then the Magician announced that the individual who had lost the most in his life, would inherit the Magician's palace.

When the King of Terra-Verde arrived home to discover Penta and the child gone, he was furious. He sought and found the woman who had falsified the messengers and had her covered with tallow and wax and then burned to death.

He then sought Penta's brother, who now was greatly remorseful for his bad behavior and went with the King of Terra-Verde to Lago-truvolo to tell the Magician of their difficult lives. Their stories told, the Magician took favor on them and asked Penta and the child to come forth. Hearing the repentance of her brother and the love of the King, Penta forgave and welcomed them all in joy and love.

The Magician said to Penta, "Put your arms between your legs and bring forth your hands once more."

Penta did as she was told and her hands reappeared. Then the Magician sent Penta's brother to reign over his own kingdom again, and the King of Terra-Verde put his brother in charge of his kingdom. This allowed the King and Penta to remain with the Magician living the rest of their days in joy and forgetting the past travails.

Let us review the steps of the Heroine's Journey in relationship to these two stories. **Table 3.2** provides an overview.

In comparing these two stories, Story #1 follows the exact path of the Heroine's Journey. Story #2 is a variation, but also follows the Heroine's Journey with the two exceptions. The first exception is that the villain appears later in the story, and the second exception is that Penta requests to have her hands cut off. There are many variations of this Heroine's Journey (see bibliography) reflecting the fact that the story flourished from the twelfth through the nineteenth centuries. There are oral recordings of the tale and literary versions found throughout the world. This indicates the Heroine's Journey resonates with audiences and has worth even today.

ACTION / RESPONSES

Each step in the Heroine's journey involves events that elicit a response from the heroine. The events, coupled with her responses to them, facilitate not only growth for the heroine, but also serve to move the storyline forward. They provide a compilation of

Table 3.2 "All Was the Way It Should Be" vs. "Penta the Handless" Comparison

Heroine	"All Was the Way It Should Be"	"Penta The Handless"
Step 1: Unprotected Innocence	There is a loss of feminine influence and protection when the mother flees and the father dies.	The parents are deceased. The brother has become king, which means he has power over his sister.
Step 2: Villain Appears	The brother takes a wife who, because of her jealousy of the maiden, becomes the villain.	The villain is Masiello's wife who sends the barrel back into the sea. (Note: this step occurs out of regular sequence – see Step 4.)
Step 3: Trauma Split	The brother cuts off the maiden's hands.	The brother decides to take Penta, his sister, for a wife. Penta has a servant cut off her hands and delivers them to her brother on a plate.
Step 4: Departure	The maiden leaves home seeking the help of strangers.	The brother puts Penta in a barrel and tosses it into the sea. Penta is rescued, but tossed back into the sea by the jealous wife.
Step 5: Wilderness 1 / Basic Needs	The maiden learns how to provide food and shelter when living in the woods.	Penta is found by King of Terra-Verde and made the handmaiden to the queen.
Step 6: Safety	The maiden marries the king and he takes care of her needs. The maiden gives birth to a son.	The queen dies and Penta marries the king. Penta brings forth a baby boy.
Step 7: Betrayal	The villain swaps the messages so that the queen mother believes she is instructed to kill her daughter-in-law and grandson. The maiden feels betrayed by King.	The notes exchanged between Penta and the king are intercepted and exchanged by Masiello's wife. Penta believes she has been betrayed by the king.
Step 8: Wilderness 2 / Recovery	The young queen grows back her hands. She is helped by the old woman in the cottage. The king returns to speak the truth and the villain is put to death.	Penta takes refuge at the magician's palace. The king discovers the truth and has Masiello's wife burned at the stake. The brother repents his advances. Penta regains her hands by magic.
Step 9: Wholeness	Queen and king remarry and rule with peace for the rest of their lives.	All is forgiven and the King of Terra-Verde and Penta rule the magician's kingdom in joy.

knowledge that allows the heroine to develop emotionally. For example, we use the story "All Was the Way It Should Be. **Table 3.3** provides an overview.

If the events do not cause a response, there is no conflict; and if there is no conflict, there is no story. In the end, the heroine can choose wisely—based on experience and knowledge—about how she wants to behave and how she wants to be treated by others. Author Jean Shinoda Bolen probably says it best in *Goddesses in Everywoman*: "To take responsibility of making the choice is crucial and not always easy. What defines the heroine is that she does it" (281).

Comparison

We will compare the two side by side now that we have described the Sword Maiden's and Heroine's Journeys. **Table 3.4** provides an overview.

Both journeys have difficult passages of transformation. They are similar in that both the sword maiden and the heroine leave home, surmount difficult trials, and are transformed in some way. The differences between the two journeys are in "the how and the why." **Table 3.5** provides an overview.

This leads us to examine how a story's structure affects its focus. We asked ourselves, "Is the same story being told using the Heroine's Journey structure as that which is being told using the Sword Maiden's Journey structure?" We think not. To test our theory, we used ATU 510 Cinderella. This is one of the most prolific folktales. It is found across cultures and continents with hundreds of variants.[7] ATU 510A Cinderella follows the Heroine's Journey and ATU 510B The Dress of Gold, of Silver, and of Stars follows the Sword Maiden's Journey. **Table 3.6** provides an overview.

7.   *Cinderella, Tales from Around the World.* Edited by Heidi Anne Heiner. SurLaLune Press, 2012.

Table 3.3 Action and Response for "All was the Way It Should Be"

Heroine	Story Events	Action	Response
Step 1: **Unprotected** **Innocence**	The father dies and the mother leaves home.	The heroine is given power and authority by her brother.	There is no one present to protect the heroine.
Step 2: **Villain** **Appears**	The brother marries an evil woman.	There are 3 trials where the brother's wife lies each time.	The heroine is vulnerable to abuse.
Step 3: **Trauma Split**	The heroine's hands are cut off.	The heroine cannot trust her brother or sister-in-law.	The heroine is helpless and does not confront her brother.
Step 4: **Departure**	The heroine refuses to stay in harm's way.	The heroine escapes into the woods.	The heroine succeeds in healing the physical wounds.
Step 5: **Wilderness 1** **/ Basic Needs**	The heroine lives in the woods.	The heroine finds food and shelter.	The heroine learns how to provide for her basic needs.
Step 6: **Safety**	The heroine marries the king.	The heroine relies on the help of others.	The heroine is given and wears silver hands.
Step 7: **Betrayal**	The king supposedly sends a message to have the heroine killed.	The sister-in-law (villain) intercepts and exchanges the messages.	The heroine retreats to the woods and is helped by a wise person.
Step 8: **Wilderness 2** **/ Recovery**	There is a re-growth of hands.	The heroine develops the skills needed to manage her own life.	The truth is uncovered and the king and heroine reunite.
Step 9: **Wholeness**	A second wedding takes place.	The brother is informed. The villain is destroyed. The marriage vows renewed.	The melding of the heroine and king (i.e. feminine and masculine energies) allow the two to rule the kingdom in peace & harmony.

Table 3.4 Sword Maiden's Journey vs Heroine's Journey Comparison

Sword Maiden	Heroine
	Step 1: Unprotected Innocence
Step 1: Call to Adventure	**Step 2:** Villain Appears
	Step 3: Trauma Split
Step 2: Threshold Crossing into the Unknown	**Step 4:** Departure
	Step 5: Wilderness 1/Basic Needs
Step 3: Tests & Helpers	**Step 6:** Safety
	Step 7: Betrayal
Step 4: Triumph	**Step 8:** Wilderness 2/Recovery
Step 5: Return and Repeat	**Step 9:** Wholeness

Table 3.5 How and Why Differences

	Sword Maiden	Heroine
How	Self to Universal Innocence to Independence Tests and Trials Serial Events	Self to Improved Self Dependence to Independence Isolation and Introspection Single Event
Why	Triumph with boon for all	Heal the Trauma / Gain Wholeness

Table 3.6 Sword Maiden's vs Heroine's Journey Comparison

Sword Maiden "Dress of Gold, of Silver, and of Stars" ATU 510B	Heroine "Cinderella" ATU 510A
Step 1: Call to Adventure The heroine delays unwanted marriage by asking for three dresses.	**Step 1: Unprotected Innocence** Cinderella's mother dies.
	Step 2: Villain Appears A cruel woman marries Cinderella's father.
	Step 3: Trauma Split The father abandons Cinderella and she becomes a servant.
Step 2: Threshold Crossing into the Unknown The heroine escapes during the night and again when she attends the balls.	**Step 4: Departure** Cinderella resigns herself to this new state of life and retreats to the kitchen.
Step 3: Tests & Helpers The heroine wears an animal skin disguise and works as a scullery maid. She removes her disguise and attends the ball.	**Step 5: Wilderness 1 / Basic Needs** Cinderella is a good servant and is isolated in her work.
	Step 6: Safety Cinderella attends the ball and has a splendid time.
	Step 7: Betrayal The clock strikes 12 am and the magic disappears. The stepmother tries to hide Cinderella from the prince.
Step 4: Triumph The prince is charmed by her grace, beauty, and wit.	**Step 8: Wilderness 2 / Recovery** Cinderella returns to a servant's role knowing she is worthy of a prince.
Step 5: Return & Repeat The heroine returns to the kitchen undiscovered and repeats going to the ball two more times. **Final triumph** She marries the prince and lives happily ever after.	**Step 9: Wholeness and Lives Happily ever after** The shoe fits. Cinderella marries the prince to live happily ever after.

Is the Same Story Being Told?

In a Cinderella story with a Sword Maiden's Journey focus, 'Cinderella' is unhappy with her circumstances in life. Throughout the story, she actively makes plans and decisions that will improve her situation. She crosses the threshold, leaving her world of privilege behind and travels into the unknown. She encounters obstacles along the way wearing an animal skin disguise, being bullied as the lowest servant in the kitchen, attending the ball three times without anyone knowing her, and successfully banters with the Prince by using riddles to truthfully answer, yet not answer, his questions. Her triumph comes not only when she obtains the token given by the Prince, but also when the Prince recognizes her as the beautiful maiden from the ball. At this point, Cinderella moves from her individual needs to the universal needs of society by accepting her role as future queen. She and the Prince live happily ever after as does the kingdom.

In contrast, in a Cinderella story with a Heroine's Journey focus, Cinderella is a child who is abandoned by her mother and father and left in the care of a cruel stepmother. If she remains in the role of scullery maid, she is emotionally stunted—a child and a victim. She depends on the kindness of others (spirits, fairies, and animals) to help her to begin to define who she is as an individual. But their actions, while good-intentioned, do not last, as this Cinderella is not yet ready to see herself as a "whole" person. It is not until the Prince arrives with the slipper, that Cinderella can stand on her own two feet and step forth to claim her own identity. The marriage symbolizes Cinderella's emotional maturity; she is now balanced in her masculine and feminine characteristics. Thus, she and the Prince live happily ever after.

Is Cinderella seen differently depending upon which way we tell the story? We think yes. In the Sword Maiden's Journey, Cinderella's focus is on the external struggle for improving her life. She actively takes steps toward her goal of a better life. She embodies masculine strength and cunning to attain her goal of becoming queen. She regains balance as she demonstrates her feminine self, wearing beautiful clothing and treasuring the token given to her by the Prince. Her marriage to the Prince facilitates Cinderella's transformation from someone with individual concerns to the role of queen with societal concerns in ruling a kingdom. This transformation ensures happiness for all as they rule together in the future years.

In the Heroine's Journey, Cinderella's focus is on the internal struggles of growing up. She is a person who, cut off from feminine support and betrayed by the masculine, uses her own tenacity and endurance to regain balance. In the end, her marriage to the Prince signifies the balance of masculine and feminine energies. They can now rule in peace and live happily ever after.

Whichever journey structure you choose when creating a story, recognize the importance of the structure. Each structure will guide you in a direction as you choose details to include in your story. Each will help you determine your focus, and your course of action as you prepare a story to tell. It is the structure that enables us to effectuate a storyline that is recognizable and relevant to the listener.

CHAPTER 4

The Importance of the Heroine's Journey

> It takes acts of self-determination and power to restore a sense
> of wholeness after abuse ... The narrative is not about her
> survival as a victim, rather it is about her journey as a committed
> traveler fully aware of her destination (Snyder 33).

WHEN WE ASKED PARTICIPANTS IN OUR WORKSHOPS to describe and
name a hero, hands shot up and answers were called out quickly:
sword wielding, strength, courage, cunning; along with names
like comic book hero Superman, Greek mythology's Hercules, *Star
Wars'* Luke Skywalker, and baseball hero Jackie Robinson. Soon a
full page of easel paper was filled with adjectives and names of both
story characters and real people. A substantial majority of workshop
participants identified with the role of hero.

When asked to describe and name a heroine, the responses
were not nearly as spontaneous as with the hero and the easel page
was only half filled. Attributes included: inner strength, endurance, and tenacity and names included: missionary Mother Teresa
of Calcutta, political figure Eleanor Roosevelt, abolitionist Harriet
Tubman, and pioneering pilot Amelia Earhart. Surprisingly few,
if any, story characters' names were offered. Although only a few
workshop participants identified with the role of the heroine, many
believed the heroine had the more difficult journey of the two with

more physical suffering, mental anguish and an overwhelming feeling of being alone. We found this last observation paradoxical in that many of the historic women named as heroines had an organization supporting them. So, were they heroines or sword maidens?

It was clear to us that very few participants saw the heroine as a positive image with which to be identified. We asked ourselves why the heroine is seen as a negative figure. Could it be, that in western culture, we prefer to slay dragons rather than tangle with our internal demons? If that is the case, it could be the reason why the Heroine's Journey is less known than the Hero's Journey. However, author Clyde W. Ford writes about the importance of validating the strength needed to survive hardship and trauma: "… in a story that transcended victimization and denial, I asked myself, 'If a single person had lived through all these experiences, how would I describe that person's life?'" (viii).

The Heroine's Journey is significant because it is the path traveled by individuals who have experienced trauma, yet do not think of themselves as victims. The path they travel is about healing the emotional split caused by the trauma, becoming whole again. Without traveling this path of recovery, the heroine may become emotionally fixed at the point of trauma remaining a victim.

Western Civilization is filled with stories of the Sword Maiden's Journey—books, news, movies, religion, politics, and art. These stories show that we must travel an adventure to achieve the goal and that happiness is found only when the desired goal is reached. There is a structural hierarchy of achievers surrounding us. Strong figures lead the country, manage corporations, run the military and scientific worlds. Given these heroic examples, we are taught to "stop whining," "buck up" and "pull up those bootstraps" when trauma occurs. For those who can compartmentalize, the injury is tucked away and the individual moves on with his/her life. For others, the trauma stays just below the surface of everyday life causing depression, fear, and anger. Those individuals stay in trauma until a paradigm shift changes their view of the world and how they see themselves in it. This paradigm shift is traveling the Heroine's Journey. The Heroine's Journey is about taking control of one's life—about no longer being a victim. It is about independence and making one's own decisions wherein the masculine and feminine energies are balanced, and the individual becomes whole.

DOROTHY'S PERSPECTIVE

My mother was ill for most of my childhood and, although I had two older sisters, most of my time was spent with my father. On evenings and weekends, I tagged along on his various jobs of plumbing, carpentry, electrical work, brickwork, and engine repair. I wore jeans and sneakers instead of dresses. I liked the fact my hands looked rough and dirty like my father's hands. I sat on the bar stool at the local tavern sipping orange soda, while he shared a beer with his friends. Other times I stood quietly listening, while he joked with other mechanics at the garage. Each Friday night, we went to the bank to deposit his weekly earnings and then to the barbershop for his haircut and more talk with the men.

I lived in a world divided by the male and female genders. Fathers went to work and mothers stayed home and made babies. I'm not sure if my father truly believed that statement, as he was proud of his three daughters' accomplishments, but my sisters and I knew without doubt that he would trade any one of us for a son. This early experience instilled the feeling of being a second-rate gender; this was the reason I tried so hard to emulate male behaviors in my business career. It was also the reason I felt empty and unsatisfied by midlife.

BARBARA'S PERSPECTIVE

I saw the Sword Maiden's Journey played out in the women around me. They were heroic, practical and worked hard. They held their own in "a man's world" and did it well.

The reality in my family was that "men die young." Due to war and heart disease, women in my family were widowed as young as twenty-five, and others in midlife with children to raise. Both of my grandmothers outlived their husbands by twenty years. The "old" men of the family were sixty-five, if that. I did not grow up with grandfathers; one died before my parents married and the other when I was six. My grandmothers were at the top of the family hierarchy—and you did not mess with them. Education was important. My maternal grandmother, though living in a rural farming community, had a high school diploma in 1913. This was a time when across the United States, half the student population did not finish the eighth grade[8] and only thirty-five percent of seventeen-year-olds were in high school.[9] She tutored my grandfather and his brothers in mathematics.

My mother, though supportive, was not a "warm-fuzzy" mom. She was all business, analytical, and no-nonsense. She and her sisters were sent to college, my uncles, their brothers, were not. I attended Catholic school and was surrounded by nuns, women in professional and administrative positions with Master's degrees, who held strong opinions and beliefs,

---

8.   Tyack, David and Cuban, Larry. *Tinkering Toward Utopia: A Century of Public School Reform.* Harvard University Press, 1995, p.69.

9.   Conant, James Bryant. *The American high school today: A first report to interested citizens.* McGraw, 1959, p.6.

and who influenced young minds. As a child and as an adult, I used the Hero's Journey model of achievement to frame my own life's story. I was not dainty and petite as the storybook princesses were depicted. I was tall, active, a tomboy who liked the idea of adventure and there was never any doubt that I would go to college and enter the workforce as a professional.

PERSONAL FRUSTRATIONS

To Dorothy's surprise when writing her thesis in 2005, if she typed the word HEROINE, Microsoft's WORD© dictionary informed her that HEROINE was a misspelling and repeatedly wanted to auto correct "heroine" to "hero". Here was a major word processing program, being used by thousands of people each day, that excluded this word.

In the Google Docs' dictionary, 'heroine' is defined as "a woman admired or idealized for her courage, outstanding achievements, or noble qualities." In the online Thesaurus by Merriam-Webster, "heroine" is not considered a word. The error message reads, "The word you've entered isn't in the Thesaurus. Click on a spelling suggestion below or try again using the search bar above."

To Barbara's surprise and frustration, throughout her career, it has been a challenge to find folktales featuring strong female protagonists. Even with the help of the Aarne-Thompson Tale Type Index and later the revised Aarne-Thompson-Uther Index to search for stories, there are only a few tale types featuring female protagonists who are capable and clever, e.g. AT 317 A Peasant Girl Rescues the Prince, ATU 451A Sister Seeking Her Brothers, AT 875 Clever Peasant Girl Solves the King's Riddles. Most of the female titles focused on the negative e.g. ATU 315 The Treacherous Sister, AT 318 The Faithless Wife or those who need saving, e.g. AT 310 Maiden in

Tower, AT 301 Quest for a Vanished Princess, AT 530 Princess on the Glass Mountain, AT 851 Princess Who Cannot Solve the Riddle.

When we began presenting the workshop on the Heroine's Journey, we found that people didn't know about this structure. We heard, "Why have I never heard about this before?" The more dramatic response has been "Oh! I've been telling a story in the wrong way. I've been telling it as a Sword Maiden's Journey. It's not!" We also discussed the ongoing need to keep talking about the Heroine's Journey because, though it is not new, it remains relatively unknown and needs to be brought into the conversation of modern storytellers. We all can learn from the experiences of women who have gone before us so that we do not forget where we have been and where we still need to go.

Experiences like these keep us steadfastly engaged in the work of presenting and clarifying the Heroine's Journey. Women who are wondering about taking the Heroine's Journey will hear that others have succeeded in their quests, and that there is help to be found for those ready to embark on their own Heroine's Journey. For those who only know the Sword Maiden's Journey, the Heroine's Journey shows another way to achieve transformation.

CHAPTER 5

Applications for the Heroine's Journey

It [storytelling] is the most basic and accessible of all our art forms. It is
an act of pure creation. It is experience and imagination made manifest
in language. It uses both sides of our brain. It invites one member of the
species to appreciate and understand another. It has the power to elicit
physical and emotional connections and response (Niemi and Ellis 50).

THE HEROINE'S JOURNEY IS NOT A STORY. It is a structure for *shaping*
a story. The use of common structures allows the reader or listener
to engage in the story efficiently because there is a known order
in which major events happen. The Sword Maiden's and Heroine's
Journeys usually follow the "Straight Narrative plot line" (Niemi,
51-59). This means that one event causes the next event to happen.
For example, the maiden's hands are cut off (event), and she flees
to the woods (event). Because we don't know *how* the events will
happen, the unknown keeps our interest in the story rather than
tracking the order of events. We have listed a sampling of contemporary elements for the Heroine's Journey structure, which you may
find helpful in recognizing life situations and creating stories. **Table
5.1** provides an overview.

Table 5.1 List of Contemporary Elements for the Heroine's Journey Structure

Heroine	Folktale	Contemporary
Step 1: Unprotected Innocence	Absence of mother and sisters causes a separation from feminine energies.	The heroine lacks protection because s/he is abandoned by family and/or community.
Step 2: Villain appears	The villain may be male or female.	The villain may be a physical person or a metaphorical entity.
Step 3: Trauma Split	A male relative cuts off the heroine's hands.	The trauma may be a physical, emotional, or metaphorical wounding.
Step 4: Departure	She leaves home.	The heroine chooses to depart from the situation/place of harm.
Step 5: Wilderness 1 / Basic Needs	She lives in the woods alone learning to find food and shelter.	Any place of solitude that affords the heroine a place of learning to care for oneself.
Step 6: Safety	She marries, usually to royalty.	Any place that offers safety or a better situation/place than where the heroine had been. The heroine is cared for by others.
Step 7: Betrayal	Her husband appears to want her killed.	A trust, whether with a person or communication, is broken.
Step 8: Wilderness 2 / Recovery	She lives in the woods again. This time she is not alone for she has the support of an old wise woman.	Any place where the heroine is transformed with the help of others.
Step 9: Wholeness	She remarries the king and rules in peace and harmony. She lives happily ever after.	The trauma is healed and the heroine is whole.

STORY DEVELOPMENT

When crafting a story to tell, there are several things to consider when deciding if the Heroine's Journey is the right structure to use.

1. Does a trauma occur to the main character?
   a. The trauma may be physical and/or emotional
   b. The wounding is caused by a male relative or other forces that have aspects of the masculine such as physical strength, cunning, or analytical thought
2. Does the main character have an emotional transformation for the better?
3. Does the main character complete all the steps of the Heroine's Journey?

This third requirement is important for the storyteller because if the main character does not achieve wholeness, the story performance can easily slip into "therapy on stage" (e.g. the teller is emotionally too close to the material or too much personal information is shared). Also by completing all the steps, there is a full storyline and it is not simply an anecdote.

Another point to consider is that of the focus of the story. As we saw in our discussion of the story of "Cinderella" in Chapter 3, a story's focus may change depending upon the structure used. Here is an example.

Barbara was thinking about creating a story about her birthing experiences. She was unsure if she wanted to use the Heroine's Journey structure or that of the Sword Maiden. By mapping the story into the different structures, it became easy to see where the story was going and which events were missing that she needed to include. Using the tables, we have developed, she could "fill in the blanks" to see how the story looked in each structure. **Table 5.2** provides an overview.

Table 5.2 "Birthin' Babies" Sword Maiden's vs Heroine's Journey

Sword Maiden	"Birthin' Babies"
Step 1: Call to Adventure	Barbara goes into labor.
Step 2: Threshold Crossing into the Unknown	She enters the labor and delivery room.
Step 3: Tests & Helpers	The nurses are her helpers during her fast labor. She pushes for three hours, but the baby is stuck. The obstetrician performs a cesarean.
Step 4: Triumph	The baby is born alive and Barbara is also alive.
Step 5: Return and Repeat	Her second birthing experience is exactly the same.

Heroine	"Birthin' Babies"
Step 1: Unprotected Innocence	Barbara had no examples of women who had difficult deliveries.
Step 2: Villain Appears	Complications are due to fast labor causing the baby to twist. The villain is Barbara's body.
Step 3: Trauma Split	After pushing for three hours, the baby is stuck.
Step 4: Departure	She chooses a C-section.
Step 5: Wilderness 1 / Basic Needs	A healthy baby is delivered.
Step 6: Safety	There is no reason to assume this will happen again so plans are made for the next birth to be vaginal birth.
Step 7: Betrayal	Fast labor again causes the baby to twist and a second C-section occurs.
Step 8: Wilderness 2 / Recovery	She allows herself to grieve the loss and disappointment of not experiencing natural childbirth.
Step 9: Wholeness	She accepts and embraces the full reality of her birthing experiences.

The story that would be told using the Sword Maiden's Journey structure is a valid version of the events, but it was not the one that accurately portrayed her experience. However, by reframing the events using the Heroine's Journey, Barbara could give voice to the highly-charged emotions she experienced following the births of her children. She also discovered that her "villain" was her own body and that she had to come to grips with being angry and disappointed in it. Whether this story is ever performed is not the issue. Going through the process of framing her experience in the Heroine's Journey brought about healing and understanding for her.

In addition to story development, the Heroine's Journey may be used in fields such as psychological therapy and business, i.e. both in individual situations and at the organizational level. Here are some examples.

PSYCHOLOGICAL THERAPY

Most therapists require their patients to tell their stories as a first-person narrative. However, in group settings or in performance, a healing story in the first person may be too difficult for the audience to embrace. Thus, third person narrative is frequently used. Dorothy also found that, with the permission of her therapist, she could use third person narrative in session when telling a painful event. While fully owning the situation, the details of the event were easier to tell when using the third person.

"CIRCLE OF TEARS" ©1996 DOROTHY CLEVELAND

The newborn baby was crying, while his 15-month old sister was sleeping in her bed. Nothing seemed to settle him; diaper changed, bottle refused, cuddling rejected. His young fragile body straightened and the wails just kept coming.

The Mother was inexperienced and exhausted. Two babies in a little over one year; lack of sleep and still recovering from birthing. She remembered her own mother. The one with the nagging voice telling her she was a bad child and using a leather belt to sting the backs of tiny legs.

And still, the baby cried. The Mother carefully placed the infant in the crib, closed the bedroom door and went downstairs to the basement. It was cold and damp in the unfinished room. The Mother huddled in the corner trying to control her anger. Then the tears came. Tears for herself, tears for her baby still wailing in the room above.

Rallying, the Mother took the steps one at a time. She opened the door to the bedroom and reached for the infant. The memories of childhood resurfaced. Her legs stung and her mother's voice whispered in her head, "You are a bad mother."

She held the infant close to her breast and sat in the rocker. Back and forth she rocked for long minutes until the cries turned from wails to whimpers. The tears came again. One for forgiveness, one for her inner child, and one for her sleeping infant. Now the anger left her heart. Both Mother and child were calm. The circle of violence had been broken; transformation occurred.

Table 5.3 provides an overview.

The events of the story do not fit well into the structure of the Sword Maiden's Journey. A goal was achieved when the baby stopped crying, but the emotional impact of abuse is not addressed in the Sword Maiden's Journey. In the Heroine's Journey, however, the steps are easily completed and the story shows the transformation of the mother. The use of this structure met the three requirements

Table 5.3 "Circle of Tears" Sword Maiden's vs Heroine's Journeys

Sword Maiden	"Circle of Tears"
Step 1: Call to Adventure	Mother is unable to calm the crying baby and she becomes angry.
Step 2: Threshold Crossing into the Unknown	She enters the dark, cold basement.
Step 3: Tests & Helpers	She needs to calm her anger.
Step 4: Triumph	She rocks the baby to sleep and is not abusive to the infant.
Step 5: Return and Repeat	She breaks the cycle of child abuse.

Heroine	"Circle of Tears"
Step 1: Unprotected Innocence	She was abused as a child by her mother.
Step 2: Villain Appears	She hears the nagging voice of her mother saying, "bad child."
Step 3: Trauma Split	The crying baby triggers memories of abuse.
Step 4: Departure	She leaves the baby in the crib and closes door.
Step 5: Wilderness 1 / Basic Needs	She retreats to the basement.
Step 6: Safety	Her tears release her pain and anger.
Step 7: Betrayal	She hears the nagging voice of her mother calling her a "bad mother."
Step 8: Wilderness 2 / Recovery	Rocking the baby, she learns patience and how to stay calm in difficult situations.
Step 9: Wholeness	Both mother and baby are calm; the cycle of abuse is broken.

of a Heroine's Journey: 1) a trauma, 2) an emotional transformation and 3) balance achieved for the main character and the writer of the story.

BUSINESS—INTERPERSONAL SITUATION

Dorothy often used story in the workplace, especially when working with employees who needed to change behavior. To make the transformation easier, she used the Heroine's Journey structure to frame the situation. Using story allowed truths to be spoken aloud in a safe setting and for the individual to objectively react to the situation. As author Annette Simmons states in *A Safe Place for Dangerous Truths*:

> If you set the stage for storytelling, people are more likely to tell their own stories ... They speak personally, they focus on process as much as content, and they back off outcome in favor of observation. For these reasons (and for reasons that I don't understand), telling a story is a safe way to address a dangerous truth (172).

Here is an example using the Heroine's Journey structure to better frame an office situation:

"MOVING ON" ©2016 DOROTHY CLEVELAND

> It had been one year since Sally had come to work at the law firm and she was experiencing difficulties. Tom, a partner with the firm and Sally's supervisor, was absent a lot and not available to answer her questions. Sally was often left alone to improvise time spent with clients and in court. In her one-year evaluation, Tom indicated that Sally was ineffective at client communication and her courtroom presence was shallow. However, he did report that she was very good at legal writing.

Sally was crushed upon reading the evaluation and complained to the Human Resource manager that she felt Tom had been unfair.

"He's never around when I need help and he's never gone to court with me or sat in on a client meeting. I don't see how he can make these remarks," Sally pouted.

The HR manager asked, "Do you like being a practicing attorney?"

Sally responded, "Yes and no. I like the research and writing, but the courtroom and clients frustrate me."

"Do you think you would do better with a different supervisor?" ask the HR manager.

"I really don't know. I haven't thought about it. All I do is work. There is no time for anything else," said Sally.

The HR manager suggested that Sally take a couple of days off to reflect on the evaluation and what it meant for her to be an attorney. Sally explained that she felt her position was at risk and the distress she was feeling would only further aggravate the stomach ulcer that had developed in the last few months.

Sally left Human Resources feeling alone and confused. She went to her apartment and fell asleep. The next morning, she went for a long walk along the river. It had been a while since she had heard the birds sing, squirrels scamper and leaves rustle. When had her life gone off track? She found a coffee shop, got herself an iced mocha and began to evaluate her life.

Her father had wanted her to be an attorney. "You'll make good money," he said. But she hated the long hours, the complaining clients and obnoxious judges. There was no beauty or rewards for her as an attorney. What she really liked was writing briefs, affidavits, motions. In writing, she could use her persuasive skills as well as tell the client's story.

By the time she returned to the HR manager, Sally had made the decision to find a position that would not give her an ulcer. The two brainstormed different occupations and, with luck and the assistance of a few phone calls, Sally soon found a position that suited her and a career in which she succeeded.

Table 5.4 provides an overview.

BUSINESS—ORGANIZATIONAL LEVEL

Working with organizations, Dorothy found that many times upper management would not listen to a story. They wanted bullet points—something short and sweet. Dorothy found that if she developed a story to better understand the issues and organize her thoughts, she then could easily translate the story into a clear and concise bullet point presentation.

While writing this book, Barbara came upon a revelation. The Heroine's Journey structure described the struggle apparent in organizations going through transition. **Table 5.5** provides an overview.

Too often organizations make it through the transition to Step 6, but had not completely matured and, therefore, continued to struggle. Realizing that the organization may be experiencing Step 7 and that it still had to work through Step 8, provides insight as to what future actions need to be taken.

Table 5.4 "Moving On" Outline

Heroine	"Moving On"
Step 1: Unprotected Innocence	Sally's father demands she become a lawyer; he ignores her desire to be a writer.
Step 2: Villain Appears	Tom gives Sally a poor evaluation.
Step 3: Trauma Split	Sally develops an ulcer.
Step 4: Departure	Sally takes off from work for a few days.
Step 5: Wilderness 1 / Basic Needs	She sleeps from exhaustion.
Step 6: Safety	She walks along the river and realizes that she's calm when away from work.
Step 7: Betrayal	Sally's career offers a good salary, but the price is long hours and an ulcer.
Step 8: Wilderness 2 / Recovery	She brainstorms with the HR person about alternative careers.
Step 9: Wholeness	She finds a new position where she can be successful and healthy.

Table 5.5 Business/Organization Outline

Heroine	Organization XYZ
Step 1: Unprotected Innocence	The organization is loosely managed.
Step 2: Villain Appears	A chief executive officer is hired. In this example, the CEO is the villain; it could be another person in the organization or an entity such as a board of directors or executive board.
Step 3: Trauma Split	The needs of the membership are ignored.
Step 4: Departure	Membership numbers decline.
Step 5: Wilderness 1 / Basic Needs	The organization reorganizes to cover the basic needs of the membership.
Step 6: Safety	The organization establishes a financial shelter or goes in a new direction.
Step 7: Betrayal	The CEO depletes the financial shelter or blocks changes.
Step 8: Wilderness 2 / Recovery	Organization re-evaluates sustainability.
Step 9: Wholeness	The membership succeeds on its own. The CEO disappears and a new CEO hired.

CHAPTER 6

The Hybrid Models

The old story is over, and the myth of the heroic quest has taken a new
turn on the evolutionary spiral … Women today are acquiring the courage
to express their vision, the strength to set limits, and the willingness
to take responsibility for themselves and others in a new way. They are
reminding the people of their origins, the necessity to live mindfully,
and their obligation to preserve life on earth (Murdock 184-185).

SOMETIMES STORIES DO NOT CLEANLY FIT INTO ONE STRUCTURE.
As we read dozens and dozens of variants of ATU 706 Girl Without
Hands, we found stories from Romania that combined both the
Sword Maiden's and the Heroine's Journeys.[10] Looking at this hybrid
structure, we saw the potential for use with historical and biograph-
ical material. This type of story is enticingly rich in images and
conflict, but can be confusing and convoluted because, after all, life
rarely fits into neat compartments. We have developed a series of
models to outline how the two structures can be combined and offer
the following examples to illustrate.

---

10.   Bărbulescu, Corneliu. "The Maiden Without Hands: AT 706 in Romanian
      Folklore". 1962, (25 variants). *Studies in East European Folk Narrative*.
      Edited by Linda Degh. American Folklore Society and the Indiana Folklore
      Monographs Series, Vol 30 no 25, 1978, pp. 319-365.

Part 1 / Part 2 Split

"Call To Arms" © 2009 Barbara Schutzgruber

I have no memory of ever thinking Dad looked deformed. He was just "Dad." To me, what was strange were the pictures of him when he was young, like the basketball picture from his high school yearbook. There he was standing tall, poised, ready to shoot, both arms extended, and equal in length. You see the man I knew did not have matching arms. His right arm was 3" shorter than his left. There was no elbow, and the arm was fused in a bent position. The hand was brown and tan, but the arm itself was pasty white in color, soft with no muscle tone, cold to the touch, and covered by a road map of scars from multiple surgeries.

I have lots of memories of watching him get ready in the morning. As a small child, I would look up and see Dad wearing dark trousers and a white, short sleeve, crew neck t-shirt. He would slip a cotton knit tube over the right arm, slide the arm into the opened topped hard protective cuff he always wore. He'd set the tongue in place and then using his left hand, he would weave those laces both at the same time, moving them back and forth, hooking them on the prongs to secure the tongue in place, like lacing up a boot. Then, using his left hand and his teeth, he would flip the laces around tying a perfect bow. All of this took well under 10 seconds. Next, he'd put on a short sleeve dress shirt, buttoned with his left hand. He would whistle as he placed a tie around his neck. And using only his left hand, he would flip the ends around tying a perfect Windsor knot. He'd put on a sport coat, pick up his large leather school satchel, and head out the door to walk the block and two houses up the hill to the high school.

It was common knowledge in my family that Dad had lost his elbow due to shrapnel in WWII, and because of this, well, he just did things differently, that's all. It was not until I was much older that I learned the story.

Gene Clarence Schutz graduated in June of 1941 from Lincoln High School, Park Falls, Wisconsin—50 miles south of Lake Superior. He entered a vocational course and worked as a machinist, saving money to take classes at Marquette University in Milwaukee.

In November 1942, he enlisted in the United States Army as a Parachute Infantry Regular. He spent three months in basic training, eleven months at Princeton University studying engineering, and fifteen months in the European Theater with the 17th Airborne Division. He was a scout in an intelligence and reconnaissance platoon, leading combat and reconnaissance patrols into enemy territory to "secure information and disrupt enemy organization."

He had thirteen jumps to his record, and the waiting never got easier, especially when the jumps were at night. The men sat facing each other in the cold belly of the plane with backs against the thin fuselage wall. The noise of the giant prop engines made it impossible to talk. They sat in the darkness, each alone with his thoughts and the glow from an occasional cigarette as they waited.

They waited for the red light to come on.

"Five seconds to drop! Ready!"

Stand. Turn. The blast of frigid wind and the red light changed to green.

"GO! GO! GO! GO! GO!"

They jumped in quick succession falling into the abyss.

On March 31, 1945, after the "jump over the Rhine," his unit came under artillery fire and his right arm was ripped to shreds. He was lucky in that he was taken by jeep to a medic station. The medic moved among the bodies of the wounded tagging limbs for amputation. His right arm was tagged. When he finally reached a hospital, medical personnel again moved among the wounded tagging and bagging belongings.

As they approached his cot, he grabbed his boots, and using his wounded arm to clutch them to his body, he said with determination, "You are not taking my jump boots," and refused to let go.

A doctor was called over, who, as it turned out, was an orthopedic surgeon.

That doctor took one look at his ability to grasp and said, "Can you squeeze my hand?"

When he did, the doctor said, "If you can do that, there's enough nerve and muscle to save the arm," and the amputation tag was removed.

For the next two years, his home was one VA hospital after another: England, New York, Colorado, Michigan. His battles continued as multiple surgeries left him fighting skirmishes with depression. At the age of 22, he had to decide how he wanted his arm for the rest of his life. In those days, there was no such thing as joint replacement, and there were only two options: fused or not fused. Fused meant the bones of his lower and upper arm would be permanently joined, either straight or bent. Not fused meant there would be a gap where the elbow used to be, with only skin and bit of sinew holding the arm together. Now always a "people person" and loving research, he began to collect data to help him make this decision. He went through the orthopedic wards talking to the other men, asking questions, listening to their stories.

Finally, he met Charlie. Charlie had lost an elbow, and his arm was not fused.

"So, what's that like?" was the question.

Charlie responded, "Well, to be honest, the arm is pretty much useless. It just hangs there limp and flops like a dead fish." And he swung that arm with a 'thump' onto the table.

"But," he said, "it's really good for getting free drinks because I can do this."

And he proceeded to take hold of his wrist, twist the lower portion of the arm 360°, then fold that arm in half—backward—in a very unnatural manner—until his hand was now resting on his shoulder. In that instant, the decision was made. The arm was getting fused!

More surgeries as bone from his left leg was taken for the grafts that would forever freeze that arm in a bent position. Because there were exposed nerves just under the skin, the slightest bump to any part of the arm would send him through the ceiling. It was like having a "funny bone" that ran the entire length of his arm, shoulder to wrist. To protect his vulnerable arm, a hard, removable "cuff" was designed. That first one was made of stiffened leather, like the armor of old.

Being completely right-handed, it was with physical and

occupational therapy that he, not only retrained his body, but rewired his brain, transferring all his right-hand abilities to his left. By the time, he was mustered out of the service in June of 1947, he could do anything with his left hand that he had ever done with his right, and he could do it just as well.

But even with all the therapy, he was still considered 80% disabled. So, the GI Bill sent him to college. He studied chemistry, mathematics, and physics. He was at the top of his class. His employment prospects were excellent. His dream job of being a research chemist was within his grasp—until the interviews. Every employer stated flatly, "It is company policy not to hire anyone with a disability greater than 40%." Shot down. And another skirmish with depression.

It was Mom who saw in Dad his natural ability to teach. There was always someone sitting at their kitchen table as he explained the latest lecture to a fellow classmate. "Why don't you go into teaching, Gene?"

And during his senior year, he changed his major to include education. In June, 1951, he graduated with a triple major in Chemistry, Mathematics, Education and a minor in Physics. For the next forty-two years, he taught high school. He taught not only the college bound, but the wood and metal shop guys, too. He taught from the perspective of the real world.

"If you're out in a boat, how do you know how deep the channel is? You look at the waves, right? Wave motion. That's physics. If you want to play pool or bowl well, learn physics. If you want to drive, maneuver, and stop a loaded pickup truck, you had better understand physics."

Over those forty-two years, he taught three generations,

meeting thousands of students. Not one of them saw him as having a "disability." He was simply Mr. Schutz.

The years, however, took their toll. He lived with a constant tingling sensation in his right arm, yet parts of the right hand were numb. Worn down over years of supporting an atrophied arm, his shoulder and back muscles deteriorated further.

As time passed, and other aspects of his physical being changed, the arm became less of a focal point. Bald by age thirty. Also by thirty, all his upper teeth had to be pulled and replaced with dentures. Over the years, there was a knee replacement, hearing loss, diabetes. And he continued to struggle with post-operative depression after bypass surgery, and a brush with possible colon cancer.

On March 23, 2000, just one week shy of fifty-five years to the day of being wounded, he seized in his sleep. 911 was called. The EMTs who came were former students. He was taken to the local hospital where he was pronounced dead. Lying on the gurney alone in that empty room, Dad looked so old and wizened. His glasses were gone. The EMTs had removed his dentures causing his upper lip to roll into his mouth. His ashen skin slackened over the bones of his face. A face that was marked with lines, blemishes and two days' worth of stubble. His entire body felt cold—as cold as that right arm had been for so many years.

The next time I saw him, he was freshly shaven and laid out in his Easter suit. The paratrooper's wings, which he always wore, were on his lapel. His wedding ring was on his left hand and a rosary was wrapped around his right. Over the next two and one-half days, more than 400 people came to pay their respects and express condolences—teachers, former students, members of the community. His obituary made the front page of the local paper. One of the men who spoke with me had been a student in one of the first classes Dad taught.

This man's face and hands told a life of hard work out-of-doors, and he simply said, "Your Dad was the first person to ever see anything in me."

Are we the sum of our parts? What if we don't have them all? How do we become whole again?

When Barbara began writing this story, she started by using the Sword Maiden's Journey model, which was fine for the first half of the story—the story of a young man going to war. But as she continued writing, she found herself struggling. There were significant elements in the full story that did not fit the Sword Maiden's Journey, and she felt as if she were trying to force a square peg into a round hole. A different structure was needed for the second half of the story. Once she switched to the Heroine's Journey structure, the rest of the story immediately fell into place. By changing the structure in the second half, she could say, "Yes, here is the story I want to tell." **Table 6.1** provides an overview.

Table 6.1 "Call to Arms" Outline

Sword Maiden	Heroine	"Call to Arms"
Step 1: Call to Adventure		The Japanese bomb Pearl Harbor.
Step 2: Threshold Crossing into the Unknown		Gene enlists in the military.
Step 3: Tests & Helpers		The Army sends him to boot camp, jump school and Princeton University.
Step 4: Triumph		He successfully completes jump school and courses at Princeton.
Step 5: Return and repeat		He has 13 successful jumps and further missions until he is wounded.
	Step 1: Unprotected Innocence	He spends two years in VA hospitals away from family and friends.
	Step 2: Villain Appears	The orthopedic surgeon, physical and occupational therapists give him hope for recovery.
	Step 3: Trauma Split	His arm cannot be restored = 80% disabled.
	Step 4: Departure	He attends college on the GI Bill.
	Step 5: Wilderness 1 / Basic Needs	He does well academically.
	Step 6: Safety	Education promises a career.
	Step 7: Betrayal	Employers refuse to hire him because of his disability.
	Step 8: Wilderness 2 / Recovery	He changes his college major.
	Step 9: Wholeness	He is a successful teacher for 42 years.

Stories do not always split neatly into "Part 1 / Part 2" structures. Sometimes one structure is embedded in the middle of the other. A story may begin in one structure, move to the other, and go back again to the original structure. To illustrate this, we have chosen two of Barbara's stories. Story #1 is her retelling of "Handless Maiden". Story #2 is her personal story "Acme Tattoo Parlor".

OVERLAPPING AND EMBEDDED
STORY #1: "HANDLESS MAIDEN"
© 2016 BARBARA SCHUTZGRUBER

Once there was a rich landowner whose wife was beautiful beyond compare. On her deathbed, she told her husband that if he married again, he should only take for his wife a woman whose beauty matched her own. As the years passed, the landowner searched for such a woman, but none could be found except for his own daughter. Hearing that her father planned to marry her, the Girl sought ways to delay the wedding. First, she asked for a robe made of gold, next for a robe made of silver, and then one made of diamonds. Taking these, she wrapped herself in a bearskin and fled into the forest where cold and hunger bit sharply into her bones and stomach.

At last she came to the court of the Green Emperor where she found work caring for the ducks and geese. Now the time had come for a series of festivals with royal feasts. The Girl went to each, first wearing the robe of gold, then the robe of silver, and finally the robe of diamonds. Each time she danced with the Emperor's son. By the third night, he had fallen in love and gave her ring. When the Girl returned to work, she asked the baker for a handful of dough to bake a loaf of bread. She took the ring the Emperor's son had given her, placed it in the dough and formed it into a loaf for baking. As luck would have it, the baker's loaves burned in the oven, so it was the

Girl's loaf that was given to the Emperor's son at the meal. Finding the ring, he called for the baker and discovered it was the Girl who had made the loaf. The Girl and the Emperor's son were married, and after a year, a child was born.

Now the landowner, having lost all his fortune, came to the court of the Green Emperor and became a servant. He recognized his daughter, now the Empress, and plotted to take his revenge. One night he crept into the bedchamber and killed her child leaving behind the blood-stained knife. The Empress was accused of the murder and condemned by her husband. Both her hands were cut off, and she and the dead child were left in the forest as prey to the wild beasts. Abandoned in the forest, she prayed to God, who healed her wounds, revived the child, and lead her to an enchanted palace where she and the child lived.

One day the Emperor was out hunting in this part of the forest and came upon the enchanted palace. He sent his servant, the poor landowner, to ask if he might roast some game. The Emperor's wife, now the Mistress of the Palace, agreed and invited the company to stay the night. In the morning, as the Emperor prepared to leave, it was made known that a golden goblet was missing. Every guest was searched and the goblet was found in the Emperor's pocket. He claimed to be innocent and knew nothing about how it came to be there, but was found guilty regardless.

The Mistress of the Palace looked at him and said, "Just as you stand in fear now, so did I when I was unfairly accused and punished."

The Emperor then recognized the Mistress as his wife and asked for her forgiveness. The truth of her father's treachery was uncovered, and he was put to death.

The retelling combines several of the Romanian versions that follow both the Heroine's Journey ATU 706 Girl Without Hands and the Sword Maiden's Journey AT 510B Dress of Gold, of Silver, and of Stars. **Table 6.2** provides an overview.

Table 6.2 illustrates the confusion that may occur when the two journeys overlap. Heroine's Steps 3-5 and Hero's Steps 1-3 can happen simultaneously with the same events.

Table 6.2 "Handless Maiden"

Sword Maiden	Heroine	"Handless Maiden"
	Step 1: Unprotected Innocence	The mother dies.
	Step 2: Villain Appears	The father cannot find a new wife.
Step 1: Call to Adventure	Step 3: Trauma Split	The father wants to marry his daughter.
Step 2: Threshold Crossing into the Unknown	Step 4: Departure	The heroine flees to forest in disguise taking with her three dresses.
Step 3: Tests & Helpers	Step 5: Wilderness 1 / Basic Needs	She becomes a servant in the emperor's household and attends three festivals/feasts wearing the dresses.
Step 4: Triumph		She is given a ring and is recognized by the emperor's son.
Step 5: Return		She marries emperor's son.
	Step 6: Safety	She becomes empress and bears a child.
	Step 7: Betrayal	She is framed by her father for killing her own child and her hands are cut off.
	Step 8: Wilderness 2 / Recovery	She is left in forest to die. She is saved and restored by God. She and her child live in the enchanted palace.
	Step 9: Wholeness and Lives Happily ever after	She confronts her husband and they are reunited. Her father is put to death.

STORY #2: "ACME TATTOO PARLOR"
© 2002 BARBARA SCHUTZGRUBER

August, 2000. On a sunny Saturday afternoon, I lay on a table in the Acme Tattoo Parlor. My hands gripping the edge, knuckles white, fire burning up my leg.

"Oh shit—this hurt!"

Another table, six years earlier. That same burning sensation—this time in the back of my hand. An IV inserted as I lay awaiting surgery—a lumbar laminectomy for a herniated disc, L5-S1.

Tears rolled down my cheek when neurosurgeon asked, "Can you envision living like this for the next five years." I was thirty-nine. I had always been active, a "tomboy" most of my life, and now my left leg was numb and useless. Unable to hold my own weight, I could barely sit for ten minutes at a time, hardly walk two blocks. I couldn't even drive the car. For four months, I tried it all—bed rest, synthetic morphine, alternating hot and cold packs, chiropractor, acupuncture, massage therapy, physical therapy, and even a series of steroid injections into my spine. I had X-rays, EMGs, MRIs and CT scans. And now it was time for the knife.

Afterward, my surgeon said the sciatic nerve looked like mushed linguine. "You will be able to function," he said, "but you'll never be like you were before. It won't be like it never happened."

And he was right. The feeling never fully returned to that leg and neither exercise nor weight training could stop the atrophy. I watched the muscle tone decay and my left calf slowly wither.

The Cincinnati Art Museum. One of the oldest in the country, massive stone pillars, huge marble steps—a bastion for the visual arts. I strolled through the galleries one summer evening surrounded by smartly dressed patrons who spoke in hushed voices as they mingled with Monet, Botticelli, Van Gogh, Picasso. In my wanderings, I came across a special exhibit. The gallery was dark, lit only by pools and pockets of light. The focus of each spotlight—single black and white photographs. I moved from shadow into light, back into shadow as I walked alone in that silent room surrounded by dozens of haunting images. Photographs of women and girls of all ages, from all parts of the world, each presented as answer to the question: "What is beauty?" I gazed at an old, old woman, her face carved deep with lines, her skin turned to leather from the sun and wind. I smiled back at the toothless grin of a little girl, hair in braids, her round face sparkling in gap-toothed transition. I looked at gnarled, twisted hands, misshapen claws molded by the ravages of hard work and arthritis.

One photograph caught my attention. A woman in her 50s with short cropped light hair. An athlete. The diagonal stripe on a runner's jersey. Arms raised, chest pushed forward as if breaking the ribbon at a finish line. As I stepped closer, I realized she was not wearing a shirt at all—and she had only one breast. The diagonal stripe—a scar from a radical mastectomy. Her body no longer symmetrical. That scar began at mid-breast bone and wrapped itself down and round her body. But woven in and through that scar was the most intricate tattoo I had ever seen. Lines, Celtic knots, vines all danced around each other creating an exquisite piece of art. The woman's face radiated victory, triumph and joy. Her arms raised up in an embrace: "I am alive, and this is me."

I turned and came face to face with Marie Antoinette. Powdered hair rising to the heavens, painted face and beauty mark, cinched waist, hooped skirt wider than her arms' reach. She was surrounded by her ladies-in-waiting: Scarlet O'Hara coquettishly peering from behind a lace fan, Miss America standing tall and regal wearing her diamond tiara, a model for Victoria's Secret seductively draped across a couch. What is beauty? Good question.

The Acme Tattoo Parlor, St. Paul, Minnesota. Two large plate glass windows bearing the words "No Appointment Necessary" and "We're Ready When You Are" flanked the door. A metal grate, capable of spanning the storefront, was pushed off to one side. As I entered, a teenage girl stood with her mother at the worn Formica counter. That girl made no attempt to mask her indignation as the employee explained in a very matter-of-fact voice that, per state law, you must be eighteen years of age to get a tattoo—regardless of parental or guardian approval. "Tough luck" was all that mother said as they walked out of the establishment.

I looked around. I had never been inside a tattoo parlor before. Signs graced walls—which were paneled in cheap wood veneer:

Acme Tattoo—The Industry Leader

Talent, Techniques, Attitude, Equipment and Hospital Sterilization

American Sign Language Interpreters available

We're the shop your parents came to

Fully licensed and insured

CPR and First Aid certified

There's no substitute for quality, safety, AND a real shiny floor

There was the grey-haired woman in her sixties getting a daisy chain tattooed around her ankle. "This is for when I go square dancing."

The owner of the shop wore shorts and a tank t-shirt. He was covered with tattoos—up his arms, onto his chest and back, down his legs. He was doing a touch up on a mermaid at the base of a gal's spine; in the next chair, her mother was getting a butterfly in purple ink on her shoulder.

A rather handsome man in his thirty, was greeted from the counter with, "What can we do for you this time?" No tattoos were visible. He asked for four names to be written in cursive script on his neck. I found myself wondering just how many names might be tattooed on that body—and where.

A young couple arrived in a quest of the perfect his and her matching tattoos. We passed the pattern books back and forth as I scanned page after page of designs. I saw images so amazing they took my breath away, and images so disturbing they made my skin crawl. At last I found it. A vine with red roses, simple and delicate, to adorn my damaged limb. I was handed a clipboard with forms to be filled out and signed. Payment by cash or credit card. No checks accepted. A woman in her forties, dressed in comfortable 'Bohemian clothing,' looking very much the artist, transferred the rub-on design to my leg. I spent a long time looking at it in the mirror. This is permanent. She said I could come back another day if I wasn't sure. I could even come back within a month, at no extra charge, if I wanted to add green to the leaves. Finally, I took a deep breath and said, "OK."

Now she did ask if I really wanted the design to begin at my bony ankle and I told her not to worry. I did not have any feeling in that leg so pain would not a problem. And I confidently climbed onto the table. She picked-up an old ceramic shaving mug. The brush clicked against its side as she whipped the soap into a frothy lather. I watched as she spread that foam on my leg, unfold an old-fashioned straight razor, and drew it back and forth on the leather strap, each time with a snap. I heard the blade scraping against my leg, and I didn't feel it. Then she picked up a gadget that looked and sounded like an engraving tool and began.

It was at this point the words "wood burning kit" took on a whole new meaning. I had grown so accustomed to being cut off and disconnected from that leg that it never occurred to me that even though surface nerves may be dead, the deep ones can work just fine! I was no longer a mere spectator for this event, I was a full contact participant.

"Sometimes pain is better than numbness," my neurosurgeon once said.

Oh yeah? Right! It is amazing how those Lamaze breathing techniques stay with you for your entire life because I was using them! As the needle moved along, my leg began to spasm. Nerves that had lain dormant for years were suddenly on stimulus overload. With reflexes that come only with years of experience, that Bohemian artist locked down a grip—gentle, but extremely firm. My leg wasn't going any anywhere. Thirty LONG minutes later, she was done. My leg was wrapped in gauze. I was given my care instructions for the next six weeks and I hobbled out into the late afternoon sun. I did NOT go back to have green added to the leaves!

What is beauty? In Cincinnati, I saw myself reflected in every one of those photographs—my past, my present, my future. Beauty? Beauty is fluid. And so is life. Both are filled with fast moving water, calm eddies, rocks, and debris. To be more than a mere spectator, to be a full contact participant in life is not easy. It takes hard work, serious commitment and a lot of endurance! That's why, just as any athlete does, I continue to train. Because I want to stand with MY arms raised up, MY face radiating with victory, triumph, and joy as I embrace life. "I am alive and this is me."

This story also begins by using the Heroine's Journey structure, changes to the Sword Maiden's Journey and then back to the Heroine's Journey. **Table 6.3** provides an overview.

The elements in this story fulfill the steps of the Heroine's Journey and the Hero's Journey, but do not overlap as shown in Table 6.2.

Tellers of convoluted folktales or writers of complicated stories must have a firm grip on the reins to keep all the horses in check! Here are a couple of hints to help when combining structures:

- If you start with the Sword Maiden's Journey and want to add the Heroine's Journey, do so at Step 3: Tests & Helpers. Complete the Heroine's Journey, and then move back to the Sword Maiden's Journey at Step 4: Triumph.

- If you start with the Heroine's Journey and want to incorporate the Sword Maiden's Journey, do so at Step 5: Wilderness I and/or Step 8: Wilderness II. Insert a complete Sword Maiden's Journey and then go back to where you left the Heroine's Journey to finish the story.

Table 6.3 "Acme Tattoo Parlor" Outline

Sword Maiden	Heroine	"Acme Tattoo Parlor"
	Step 1: Unprotected Innocence	Barbara prefers the life of a "tomboy" rather than spending time with women.
	Step 2: Villain Appears	Her body (as the villain) appears strong, but it isn't.
	Step 3: Trauma Split	The herniated disc crushes the sciatic nerve and she is unable to walk.
	Step 4: Departure	She makes choices for treatment.
	Step 5: Wilderness 1 / Basic Needs	She undergoes the different treatments.
	Step 6: Safety	The surgery is successful, but she must wait to see how much function will return to her leg.
	Step 7: Betrayal	The leg remains numb and neither exercise nor weight training can stop the atrophy.
	Step 8: Wilderness 2 / Recovery	She visits the Cincinnati Art Museum.
Step 1: Call to Adventure		She sees the photo of a woman with a tattoo.
Step 2: Threshold Crossing into the Unknown		She enters the tattoo parlor.
Step 3: Tests & Helpers		The tattoo artist offers guidance. Barbara must pass the test of withstanding pain.
Step 4: Triumph		The tattoo is complete.
Step 5: Return		The tattoo now adorns the damaged limb.
	Step 9: Wholeness and Lives Happily ever after	She is now committed to being a full contact participant in life and embraces who she is.

If this were not confusing enough, we have found that the Sword Maiden's Journey AND the Heroine's Journey can be happening at the same time—with two different characters within the story. The following story is an example of this situation.

PARALLEL
"ACROSS THE TRACKS" © 2004 DOROTHY CLEVELAND

It was a pleasant summer morning, and the fine white sand in my sandbox was wet from last night's rain. I was mixing a pretend cake with an old silver spoon using a Cadillac hubcap for a bowl. I heard the screen door slam. When I looked up, there stood Mother.

"Come," she said. "We are going on a visit."

I looked at her with wonder. Mother had not been visiting since father decided to transplant the family from the city to the woods. And I'm talking woods—dirt road, no running water, no indoor plumbing. Besides, we only had one neighbor, Mrs. Trieb, the recluse who lived across the tracks.

Two sets of steel rails wound their way through a deep ravine covered with sumac, itch weed, goldenrod, and sticker bushes. The near side of the ravine was a small hill, but to me it looked huge. Mother held my hand tightly, tugging me upwards when my footing gave way. Halfway down, Mother stopped to show me how to turn my feet sideways and dig into the sandy soil to keep from slipping.

"If your father hadn't taken us from the city, we would be on the trolley with my sisters and your cousins going shopping instead of traipsing in this God-forsaken wilderness."

At the bottom of the hill were the two sets of train tracks.

Black ties of old wood. Steel rails. Rusty spikes. River rock piled in between. We crossed one set of tracks before stopping to catch our breath. My legs shook. Mother had sufficiently scared me about the trains that wound through the country-side. Not so long ago, a stray dog had run too close to the tracks and a freight train had sucked him under. Mother told me that's what would happen to me if I ever went near the tracks.

Just then, a train whistle sounded in the distance, and the ground beneath our feet began to tremble. Mother tugged at my hand. We leapt across the other track and began climbing. We made it a quarter of the way up the hill when the train whizzed by. Mother pushed me against the earth until the train passed. My heart beat fast feeling the mighty tug of the train. Then, as quickly as it had begun, it was over. The ground once more still, we continued our climb.

When we reached the top of the other side, we stopped to empty the dirt from our shoes and pull prickly stickers from our socks. The white rubber toes of my KEDS had black smudges from the tracks. Mother spit and rubbed, but the grease just smeared. Heaving a sigh, she smoothed my hair and shirt trying her best to make me look presentable for Mrs. Trieb.

Mrs. Trieb lived in a white, wood-frame house. The unruly front yard was tall with wild grass. A large black crow, perched on the roof, greeted us with a loud caw. We went around to the back of the house and knocked on the screen door.

Mother shouted, "Mrs. Trieb, do you mind a visit?"

An old woman appeared in the doorway.

"Come in. I'm fixing tea."

I peered around Mother's leg to see Mrs. Trieb. Her torso, permanently bent forward at the waist, had to twist up and to the right to see into Mother's face. She wore a black dress with a high collar and long sleeves; over the dress was a navy blue apron. She was a tiny woman with delicate features and striking black eyes and pointed nose. She wore her wispy gray hair twisted into a tight knot upon her head.

The room was small, the air thick and stale. A kerosene lantern dimly lit the space. Mother took a seat at the table, and Mrs. Trieb pointed to a stool next to the potbelly stove for me. Mrs. Trieb offered cookies; I waited for Mother's nod of approval before taking a small bite, and then another and another, for the cookies tasted good. I looked around the room; an archway directly across from me led to her bedroom. There was a rocking chair with an embroidered pillow and an iron bed with a crazy quilt smoothed over a sagging mattress. An edge of the drawn shade had rolled with age, allowing a stream of sunlight into the room. A single crystal hung from the center of the archway. The sunbeam pierced the crystal, sending dancing rainbows along the gloomy walls.

I watched the rainbows as the two women chatted. I had heard Mother tell this story many times before.

"The days take so long to pass. I have scrubbed the house until my knuckles bleed. My husband leaves early, comes home late, and then works on the house. We barely talk. My two older girls are busy with school and their friends. If we lived near the city, there would be things for me to do. Then there is this one," Mother nodded in my direction, "I don't know what to do with this one. I'm not as young as I used to be and when the Curse comes, I'm so weak I can barely get out of bed."

Mrs. Trieb placed her teacup upon the saucer. "The woods are not so bad, they can be a healing place and really are quite beautiful. You just don't know how to see it. Once you do, you will feel rooted again. Come," she patted Mother's hand, "let us walk through my garden."

Outside we squinted at the brightness. Mrs. Trieb put on a black straw hat and secured it with a long hatpin piercing through the topknot of her gray hair. She grabbed a hoe to steady herself as we walked. The garden was twice the size of her house. She had corn, green beans, peas, wild asparagus, a few potatoes, tomatoes, cabbage, strawberries, and raspberries. She had sunflowers, wild roses, iris, gladiolas, tiger lilies, violets, pansies, honeysuckle, daisies, even parsley, rosemary, and chives, all planted in neat rows with room to walk between.

When we came upon a dark maroon-colored plant, Mother asked, "What's that?"

"Ah, I call it Purple Passion."

Mrs. Trieb cut a couple of slips. She put the cuttings into Mother's hand.

"Take these for your garden," said Mrs. Trieb.

"But I don't..." began Mother.

Mrs. Trieb, clasping her hands around Mother's, strained her twisted body upward to stare deeply into Mother's eyes.

"Start one. Search the woods for the plants you favor; leave behind those you do not. The house you must share with husband and children. The garden is your own. Make of it what you will."

Then Mrs. Trieb moved from Mother to me. Placing her hands firmly on my shoulders, Mrs. Trieb said to Mother, "And don't fret about this one. The woods will teach her what she needs to know."

Mother took a handkerchief from her pocket and carefully wrapped the slips. When we got home, she put the slips Mrs. Trieb had given her into a glass of water. She told me that if we put the glass on the windowsill, we could watch the roots grow. When the roots were long enough, she would start a garden of her own. She turned on the radio and began humming to the music. She pulled a tablet from the drawer and began sketching her garden—a project of her own.

I went outside to my sandbox; it seemed so small now. I looked across the tracks and Mrs. Trieb was working in her garden. Her voice echoed in my head, "And don't fret about this one. The woods will teach her what she needs to know."

It was Tuesday; Mother would be ironing all afternoon. She wouldn't even know I was gone if I was back in time for supper. I walked to the edge of the yard. I had never been in the woods alone before. A large black crow swooped around me and landed on a nearby branch.

The bird cocked a black eye towards me and cawed as if to say, "Go on. It will be all right."

I had survived the trip across the tracks and now I had the courage to move outside my little world. I took a deep breath— and stepped into the woods!

Dorothy developed this story to explore two equally significant journeys, the Sword Maiden's and the Heroine's, traveled by two separate characters. She carefully wove the story to regard each journey as recognizable and important. **Table 6.4** provides an overview.

The Hybrid structures are wonderful options for creating stories because of the range of combination possibilities. Do not be afraid to experiment. Audiences will respond positively when rich content is well crafted. Sword Maiden's and Heroine's Journey story structures may also assist in comprehending larger pieces of work such as *The Kalevala, The Iliad, The Mabinogi, The Prose Edda,* and *War and Peace.*

Table 6.4 "Across the Tracks" Outline

Sword Maiden "Dorothy"	Heroine "Mother"
Step 1: Call to Adventure Mother says, "We're going visiting."	**Step 1: Unprotected Innocence** Mother is happy living in the city with her siblings.
	Step 2: Villain Appears Her husband moves the family to the woods.
	Step 3: Trauma Split Living alone in the woods brings on Mother's depression.
Step 2: Threshold Crossing into the Unknown Dorothy crosses the railroad tracks.	**Step 4: Departure** Mother decides to visit Mrs. Trieb.
Step 3: Tests & Helpers Dorothy survives the passing train. Mother, Mrs. Trieb and the crow are helpers.	**Step 5: Wilderness 1 / Basic Needs** Mother has tea with Mrs. Trieb.
	Step 6: Safety Mother wanders through the garden with Mrs. Trieb.
	Step 7: Betrayal Mother cannot stay in the garden; Mrs. Trieb sends her home.
Step 4: Triumph Dorothy crosses the tracks a second time.	**Step 8: Wilderness 2 / Recovery** Mother starts planning her own garden.
Step 5: Return and Repeat Dorothy arrives home safe and sound. The crow is calling for another adventure.	**Step 9: Wholeness and Lives Happily ever after** Mother's depression is lifted; she is happy living in the woods with her garden.

Chapter 7
Celebration and Sending Forth

> The male perspective may view success as life's goal, and thus death
> as a failure to hang on longer, to climb one final mountain … But
> the feminine perspective is that of Isis and Demeter summoning
> the crops each year, of Ishtar and Inanna mourning their dead
> boy-kings, only to welcome them the following season. Life is
> cyclical, regenerating in an unending spiral of faith and acceptance.
> With each generation comes new talents and knowledge, new
> streams branching from life's churning river (Frankel 294).

WHAT DOES THE HEROINE'S EMOTIONAL TRANSFORMATION *feel*
like at the end of her Journey? She feels strong and substantial and
powerful. Her strength is mightier than any battle sword. The earth
has supported every step of the journey creating a potent connection
between the heroine and all that is nature. She has become resilient
and can find comfort even while living in a world of paradox. She
trusts that personal values will not fail her even in times of darkness.
In achieving a higher level of sovereignty, she finds peace and happiness. As demonstrated in the personal stories we have included here,
the phenomenon of transformation transcends fictional stories. We
have experienced it within our lives, and we have heard similar
stories of emotional transformation from others who have walked
the Heroine's Journey.

What does the Heroine's emotional transformation *look* like at the end of her Journey? She acknowledges that there is always a choice—the ability to make one's own decisions about how to handle situations. She reflects on experiences. She does not berate herself about failures, but rather accepts the wisdom acquired. She makes decisions based upon the unity of mind, heart, and soul. She is part of a larger community and demonstrates the willingness to listen to others without judging them. She realizes that there are times to be quiet. She makes a conscious decision not to tell everything and refrains from adding her own two cents.

These tools were lacking in each protagonist (fictional or real) prior to experiencing the Heroine's Journey. It would be wrong to imply that the result of each journey is perfection. There will always be more journeys to attend, but each new journey will go more smoothly because of her prior experiences. She also can see where she is in the Steps. She recognizes the villain more quickly. She does not wallow in Wilderness 1; rather, she uses the time there to ponder the situation so that transformation occurs sooner and without a debilitating depression. She learns to enjoy the time spent in Safety because it is nice sometimes to have someone take care of her, while she rests. She grows and recovers in Wilderness 2 because she knows sovereignty and Wholeness will come once again.

Using the Heroine's Journey to achieve balance has worked for us. We challenge you to see if it works for your stories. Here are the steps in the process:

1. Acknowledge the differences between the Heroine's Journey and the Sword Maiden's Journey
2. Find a story that has meaning for you whether it is a fairy tale, a biography, or one of your own creation
3. Use **Table 7.1** to map out the story
4. Decide which structure to use
5. Celebrate your heroine's transformation!

Table 7.1 Sample Worksheet

Sword Maiden	
Step 1: Call to Adventure	
Step 2: Threshold Crossing into the Unknown	
Step 3: Tests & Helpers	
Step 4: Triumph	
Step 5: Return and Repeat	

Heroine	
Step 1: Unprotected Innocence	
Step 2: Villain Appears	
Step 3: Trauma Split	
Step 4: Departure	
Step 5: Wilderness 1 / Basic Needs	
Step 6: Safety	
Step 7: Betrayal	
Step 8: Wilderness 2 / Recovery	
Step 9: Wholeness	

The development of stories and performance is a venture not to be taken lightly. It takes time to process what is happening in the story and what the meaning of the story is for the teller. There is the work of plot and character development, and what kind of story (comedy, drama) will feed the audience's interest. We encourage you to tell as often as you can and there are story resources for you in the bibliography. Go beyond the Sword Maiden stories of adventure. Look to the stories of courageous women and men who have fought through trauma to make change. Let their stories be told!

Bibliography and Reading List

"Active Heroines in Folktales for Children"
  http://www.sisterschoice.com/heroines.html
  "Active Heroines in Folktales for Children" is updated from
  Just Enough to Make a Story: A Sourcebook for Storytellers by
  Nancy Schimmel (Sisters' Choice, 1992).

*A Dictionary of British Folk-Tales in the English Language Part A
  Folk Narratives Volume I.* Edited by Katherine M. Briggs.
  Routledge and Kegan Paul, 1970, 201-202.

"A Lady Without Hands." *How Did The Bear Originate? Folktales
  from Mongolia.* Edited by Professor Choi Luvsanjav and Dr.
  Robert Travers. Translated by Damdinsurengyn Altangerel.
  State Publishing House, Ulaanbaatar, 1988, 120-124.

"Anecdote of a Charitable Woman (Night 348)." *The Arabian
  Nights' Entertainments.* Translated by Edward W. Lane.
  Routledge, Warne, and Routledge, 1865, 455-456.

Bărbulescu, Corneliu. "The Maiden Without Hands: AT 706 in
  Romanian Folklore." 1962, (25 variants). *Studies in East
  European Folk Narrative.* Edited by Linda Degh. American
  Folklore Society and the Indiana Folklore Monographs
  Series, Vol 30 no 25, 1978, 319-365.

Barsh, Joanna and Cranston, Susie. Lewis Geoffrey. *How
  Remarkable Women Lead: The Breakthrough Model for Work
  and Life.* Crown Business, 2009.

"Biancabella and the (Enchanted) Snake (Night 3 Tale 3)."
  The Facetious Nights by Straparola Volume I. Francesco
  Straparola. Translated by W. G. Waters. Illustrated by Jules
  Garnier and E.R. Hughes, Privately Printed for Members of
  the Society of Bibliophiles, 1901, 302-339.

"Blessing or Property." *Swahili Tales as Told by Natives of Zanzibar.* Translated by Edward Steere. Bell and Daldy, 1870, 391-409.

Bolen, M.D., Jean Shinoda. *Goddesses in Everywoman: A New Psychology of Women.* Harper & Row, Publishers, Inc., 1984.

"Boots and the Troll." *Popular Tales from the Norse.* George Webbe Dasent. Edmonston and Douglas, 1859, 247-254.

Campbell, Joseph. *The Hero with a Thousand Faces.* Bollingen Ser. XVII. Princeton University Press, 1973.

Chinen, M.D., A. B. "'The Handless Woman: Healing and Wilderness." *Waking World: Classic Tales of Women and the Heroic Feminine.* Penguin Putnam Inc., 1997, 97-111

Chinen, M.D., Allan B. *Beyond the Hero: Classic Stories of Men in Search of Soul.* G.P. Putnam's Sons, 1993.

Cinderella, Tales from Around the World. Edited by Heidi Anne Heiner. SurLaLune Press, 2012.

Cleveland, Dorothy. *Beyond the Sword Maiden: A Woman's Journey to Leadership through Story.* University of Minnesota MLS Master Thesis, 2005.

Conant, James Bryant. *The American High School Today: A First Report to Interested Citizens.* McGraw-Hill, 1959.

Cunningham, Elizabeth. *How to Spin Gold: A Woman's Tale.* Station Hill Openings, 1997.

"Daughter Doris." Scottish Traditional Tales. Track 2 as told by Kintyre Davie Stewart. 1955. http://www.electricscotland.com

Davis, Elizabeth and Leonard, Carol. *The Circle of Life: Thirteen Archetypes for Every Woman.* Celestial Arts, 2002.

"Dionigia and the King of England." *The Pecorone of Ser Giovanni (Tenth Day, Novel 1).* Translated by W. G. Waters. Privately Printed for members of the Society of Bibliophiles, 1901, 73-90.

"Doña Bernarda." *The Folklore of Spain in the American Southwest: Traditional Spanish Folk Literature in Northern New Mexico and Southern Colorado.* Aurelio M. Espinosa. Edited by J. Manuel Espinosa. University of Oklahoma Press, 1985, 179-180.

Ellis, Elizabeth. *From Plot to Narrative: A Step-by-Step Process of Story Creation and Enhancement.* Parkhurst Brothers, 2012.

Estes, Ph.D., Clarissa Pinkola. *Women Who Run with the Wolves: Myths and Stories of the Wild Woman Archetype.* Ballantine Books, 1992

Fearless Girls, Wise Women & Beloved Sisters: Heroines in Folktales from Around the World. Edited by Kathleen Ragan. W.W. Norton & Company, Inc., 2000.

Ford, Clyde W. *The Hero With An African Face.* Bantam Books, 1999, viii-ix.

Fournies, Ferdinand F. *Coaching for Improved Work Performance.* Liberty House, 1978, 1987.

Frankel, Valerie Estelle. *From Girl to Goddess: The Heroine's Journey through Myth and Legend.* McFarland & Company, Inc., 2010.

Gargiulo, Terrence L. *Stories at Work: Using Stories to Improve Communication and Build Relationships.* Praeger Publishers, 2006.

Goodrich, Norma Lorre. *Heroines.* HarperCollins, 1993.

Goss, Theodora. Essay "Into the Dark Forest: The Fairy Tale Heroine's Journey." 8/14/2016. https://theodoragoss.com/2016/08/14/into-the-dark-forest-the-fairy-tale-heroines-journey/

Gould, Joan. *Spinning Straw into Gold: What Fairy Tales Reveal about the Transformations in a Woman's Life.* Random House Trade Paperbacks, 2006.

"Hairy Rouchy." *The Fireside Stories of Ireland*. Patrick Kennedy. Glashan & Gill, 1875, 3-9.

Hall, Nora. *The Moon & The Virgin: Reflections on the Archetypal Feminine*. Illustrations by Ellen Kennedy. Harper & Row Publishers, 1980.

Harding, M. Esther. *The Way of All Women*. Shambhala, 1990.

Haven, Kendall. *Story Proof: The Science Behind the Startling Power of Story*. Libraries Unlimited, 2007.

Heilbrun, Carolyn G. *Reinventing Womanhood*. W.W. Norton & Company, 1979.

"John and Mary, or the Girls with the Chopped-off Hands." *It's Good To Tell You: French Folktales from Missouri*. Rosemary Hyde Thomas. University of Missouri Press, 1981, 133-138.

Johnson, Robert A. *She*. Revised Edition. Mills House, 1989.

Johnson, Robert A. *The Fisher King & the Handless Maiden: Understanding the Wounded Feeling Function in Masculine and Feminine Psychology*. HarperCollins, 1995.

Jung, C. G. *The Archetypes and the Collective Unconscious*. 2nd Edition. Translated by R.F.C. Hull. Bollingen Series XX. Princeton University Press, 1969.

Kawai, Hayao. *The Japanese Psyche: Major Motifs in the Fairy Tales of Japan*. Translated by Hayao Kawai and Sachiko Reece. Spring Publications, Inc., 1988.

Levine, Suzanne Braun. *Inventing the Rest of Our Lives: Women in Second Adulthood*. Penguin Group, 2006.

"Maiden Without Hands." *The Original Folk and Fairy Tales of the Brothers Grimm: The Complete First Edition*. Translated and Edited by Jack Zipes. Princeton University Press, 2014, 99-103.

"Mally Whuppie." *A Dictionary of British Folk-Tales in the English Language, Part A Folk Narratives Volume I.* Edited by Katherine M. Briggs. Routledge & Kegan Paul, 1970, 400-403.

"Maol A Chliobain." *Popular Tales of the West Highlands Orally Collected, Volume I.* Translated by J. F. Campbell. Alexander Gardner, 1890. #17 (4 variants), 259-274.

"Molly Whuppie." *English Fairy Tales.* 3rd Edition. Collected by Joseph Jacobs. P. Putnam's Sons, 1898, 130-135.

Murdock, Maureen. *The Heroine's Journey: A Woman's Quest for Wholeness.* Shambhala, 1990.

"Mutsmag." *Grandfather Tales: American English Folk Tales.* Selected and Edited by Richard Chase. Houghton Mifflin Company, 1948, 40-51.

Nelson, Gertrud Mueller. *Here All Dwell Free: Stories to Heal the Wounded Feminine.* Fawcett Columbine/Ballantine Books, 1991.

Niemi, Loren. *The Book of Plots.* 2nd Edition. Llumina Press, 2012.

Niemi, Loren and Ellis, Elizabeth. *Inviting the Wolf In: Thinking About Difficult Stories.* August House Publishers, Inc., 2001.

"Olive." Italian Folktales. Selected and Retold by Italo Calvino. Translated by George Martin. Harcourt, Inc, 1980, 255-261.

Paradiz, Valerie. *Clever Maids: The Secret History of The Grimm Fairy Tales.* Basic Book, 2005.

Pearson, Carol S. *Awakening the Heroes Within: Twelve Archetypes to Help Us Find Ourselves and Transform Our World.* HarperCollins, 1991.

Pearson, Carol S. *The Hero Within: Six Archetypes We Live By.* HarperCollins, 1986, 1989.

"Penta the Handless." *Il Pentamerone*. Giovanni Batiste Basile. Translated by Sir Richard Burton. Reprinted from the 1893 edition, University Press of the Pacific, 2003, 206-216.

"Polly, Nancy, and Muncimeg." *Sang Branch Settlers, Folksongs and Tales of a Kentucky Mountain Family*. Leonard Roberts. The University of Texas Press for the American Folklore Society, Volume 61, 1974. #108, 228-232.

"Queen Julika." Essay "Folklore Thursday: The Slightly Less Handless Maiden." 9/1/2016. Translated by Csenge Virág Zalka. http://multicoloreddiary.blogspot.com/2016/09 /folklore-thursday-slightly-less.html

Raffa, Ed.D., Jean Benedict. *The Bridge to Wholeness: A Feminine Alternative to the Hero Myth*. LuraMedia, 1992.

"Rebeka." Essay "Folklore Thursday: Rebeka: Girl versus Dragon." 9/15/2016. Translated by Csenge Virág Zalka. http://multicoloreddiary.blogspot.com/2016/09/folklore -thursday-girl-versus-dragon.html

Simmons, Annette. *A Safe Place for Dangerous Truths: Using Dialogue to Overcome Fear and Distrust at Work*. AMACON, 1999.

Simmons, Annette. *The Story Factor: Inspiration, Influence, and Persuasion Through the Art of Storytelling*. Revised Edition. Basic Books, 2006.

Snyder, Midori. "The Hero's Journey." *The Armless Maiden and other Tales for Childhood's Survivors*. Edited by Terri Windling. Tom Doherty Associates, Inc. 1995, 33

Tang, Camy. *Story Sensei Heroine's Journey worksheet: Make your story resonate emotionally*. Camy Tang Books, 2014.

"The Armless Maiden." *Russian Fairy Tales*. 2nd Edition. Translated by Norbert Guterman (from the collections of Aleksandr Afanas'ev). Illustrated by Alexeieff, Alexandre. Pantheon Books, 1975, 294-299.

The Armless Maiden and Other Tales for Childhood's Survivors. Edited by Terri Windling. Tom Doherty Associates, Inc., 1995.

"The Cruel Stepmother." *A Dictionary of British Folk-Tales in the English Language, Part A Folk Narratives Volume I.* Edited by Katherine M. Briggs. Routledge and Kegan Paul, 1970, 197-200.

"The Falcon's Daughter." *Folktales Told Around the World.* Richard Dorson, ed. University of Chicago Press, 1975, 159-163.

"The Girl With No Hands." *Green Hills of Magic: West Virginia Folktales from Europe.* In Ruth Ann Musick. Illustrated by Archie L. Musick. University of Kentucky Press, 1970, 139-44.

"The Girl Without Any Hands." *Tales from the Cloud Walking Country.* Marie Campbell. University of Georgia Press, 1958, 163-65.

"The Girl Without Arms." *Folktales of Japan.* Edited by Keigo Seki, Translated by Robert J. Adams. University of Chicago Press, 1963. , 98-104.

"The Girl Without Hands." Folktales of Germany. Edited by Kurt Ranke. Translated by Lotte Bauman. University of Chicago Press, 1966, 84-89.

The Great Fairy Tale Tradition: From Straparola and Basile to the Brothers Grimm. Selected, Translated, and Edited by Jack Zipes. W. W. Norton and Company, 2001, 406-415.

The Great Fairy Tale Tradition: From Straparola and Basile to the Brothers Grimm. Selected, Translated, and Edited by Jack Zipes. W. W. Norton and Company, 2001, 507-511.

The Maid of the North: Feminist Folk Tales from Around the World. Ethel Johnston Phelps, ed. Henry Holt and Company, 1982.

"The Maiden Without Hands." *The Complete Fairy Tales of the Brothers Grimm*. 3rd Edition. Translated by Jack Zipes. Bantam Books, 2003, 109-113.

"The Maiden Without Hands." Giambattista Basile. *The Great Fairy Tale Tradition: From Straparola and Basile to the Brothers Grimm*. Selected, Translated, and Edited by Jack Zipes. W. W. Norton and Company, 2001, 512-518.

"The One-Handed Girl." *The Lilac Fairy Book*. Edited by Andrew Lang. Longmans, Green, and Co., 1910, 185-208.

The Queen's Mirror: Fairy Tales by German Women, 1780-1900. Edited and Translated by Shawn C. Jarvis and Jeannine Blackwell. University of Nebraska Press, 2001.

"The Romance of Manekine." *Manekine, John and Blonde, and "Foolish Generosity"*. Philippe De Remi. Translated by Barbara N. Sargent-Baur. Pennsylvania State University Press, 2010, 13-105.

"The Story of Mariam." *100 Armenian Tales and Their Folkloristic Relevance*. Collected and Edited by Susie Hoogasian-Villa. Wayne State University Press, 1966, 253-255.

"The Turkey Hen." *Italian Folktales*. Selected and Retold by Italo Calvino. Translated by George Martin. Harcourt, Inc, 1980, 494-500,

"The Woman with Her Hands Cut Off." *Folktales of France*. Edited by Genevieve Massignon. Translated by Jacqueline Hyland. The University of Chicago Press, 1968, 116-120.

"The Woman Whose Hands Were Cut Off for Giving Alms to the Poor (Night 348)." *The Book of A Thousand Nights and A Night, Volume IV*. Richard F. Burton. The Burton Club for Private Subscribers Only, 1885, 281-283.

Thompson, Stith. *Motif-Index of Folk-Literature: A Classification of Narrative Elements in Folktales, Ballads, Myths, Fables, Mediaeval Romances, Exempla, Fabliauz, Jest-Books and Local Legends (Volume 1-6)*. Indiana University Press, 1966.

Treat, Jane and Geha, Ed.D., Nancy. *Women & Middlehood: Halfway Up the Mountain*. Balboa Press, 2013.

Tyack, David and Cuban, Larry. *Tinkering Toward Utopia: A Century of Public School Reform*. Harvard University Press, 1995.

Von Franz, Marie-Louise. *Problems of the Feminine in Fairytales*. 8th Printing. Spring Publications, Inc., 1988.

Walker, Barbara G. *Feminist Fairy Tales*. HarperCollins, 1996.

Women in Celtic Myth: Tales of Extraordinary Women from the Ancient Celtic Tradition. Retold and Explained by Moyra Caldecott. Destiny Books, 1992.

World Folktales, A Scribner Resource Collection. Atelia Clarkson and Gilbert B. Cross. Charles Scribner's Sons, 1980, 54-58.

Reader Extras

QUESTIONS AND ANSWERS WITH AUTHORS
DOROTHY CLEVELAND AND
BARBARA SCHUTZGRUBER

BEYOND THE SWORD MAIDEN: A Storyteller's Introduction to the Heroine's Journey is a 'how to' book for anyone who wants to share a story about personal perseverance, survival and transformation.

A Sword Maiden is a female who follows the hero's path of external achievement. Both of us grew up with the stories of slaying the dragon, coming face to face with the giant, fighting the battle and winning the prize, but as we moved through life this storyline didn't always fit when dealing with the real-life issues of injury, illness, divorce, or death. These life struggles are about survivors, not winning heroes. That's why our book looks BEYOND the Sword Maiden to the Heroine's Journey.

Q **What is the Heroine's Journey?**
A Heroine is anyone, male or female, who travels the path of survival and internal emotional growth and transformation. The Heroine's Journey is a formula that can be used to tell the stories of individuals who have experienced trauma and betrayal, but come out on the other side ready and able to 'live happily ever after.'

Q **Is this a new idea?**
The formula of the Heroine's Journey is not new. It can be found around the world in folktales going back centuries. The term is used today, in the fields of counseling and therapy, when dealing

with recovery from severe trauma.

Q Why is it important?

The Heroine's Journey is important because it is the path traveled by those who see themselves, not as victims, but as survivors. Too often we only hear the stories of Sword Maiden Heroes who win battles and bring home the prize of having and doing it all. But as we know, life isn't always like that. When we hear folktales, contemporary fiction and especially stories of real people traveling the Heroine's Journey, we see that others have walked life's rough path and it is possible to come out on the other side.

Q How does your book work?

We used the elements in the folktale, *The Handless Maiden,* to create general steps that a main character will undergo in the story. We developed templates that can be used for mapping the details of the story and we have sample stories to illustrate its use in different situations.

Q What kind of stories do you have in the book?

We have traditional folktales and contemporary personal stories that validate the process of emotionally maturing and healing after trauma and betrayal. All the main characters in the stories, whether male or female, survive difficult times and find happiness. For example, Barb tells a story about her father who lost the use of his right arm when wounded in WWII and the physical, emotional and societal challenges he had to overcome to lead a fulfilled life.

Q How did the two of you come to write the book together?

We've been friends for a long time—both of us are storytellers who like stories about strong women. Dorothy began working on this idea in 2004 in her master's thesis and in talking with other story-tellers. Barb saw a need for a universal structure that can be used with these types of transformational stories. Even though we have different styles of working and live 600 miles apart, we decided to collaborate on the book. We worked using shared documents via the cloud and scheduled trips to work face-to-face. We gave workshops at different storytelling conferences around the country. Each time we presented, we learned what needed more clarification and what wasn't necessary.

Q Would you do it again?

Barb: Yes! Working collaboratively helped keep me focused and staying on track. It broadened my perspective on a topic I was passionate about. It's much nicer to have someone to bounce off ideas with —especially when writer's block would rear its ugly head.

Dorothy: Informing others of the Heroine's Journey is my life's passion. There is a lack of such stories in this world and I believe our book will make a difference in helping others to create stories to share and for their personal use. Collaboration with Barb gave the book focus, organization and folklore research, which was essential for completing a quality product. I most certainly would do it again.

Q What would you like to see happen as a result of your producing this book?

Our hope is that the Heroine's Journey formula will allow more stories of recovery and wholeness to come forth. Trauma is relevant today. Women, as well as men, struggle to live happily, but with only heroic examples as a model, the lesson becomes, "stop whining," "buck up" and "pull up those bootstraps." The Heroine's Journey story gives voice and validation to the emotional reality that is part of being a survivor. Individuals wanting to enhance their lives will also find the steps in the book easy to follow. Storytellers, writers, therapists, and counselors can use the Heroine's Journey to enlighten listeners, readers and clients to live another way.

Biographies of Authors

Dorothy Cleveland tells folktales and personal stories of strong women and the shadow of life using humor and insight. For over twenty-two years, she has performed, produced storytelling events and workshops, and has served on the board for local and national storytelling organizations. She has a Masters of Liberal Studies in Leadership for Women through Story from the University of Minnesota. Dorothy also has a business resume including forty-five years of work in the administrative, human resource, finance, and managerial fields focusing in legal organizations. Dorothy's website is: http://www.beyondswordmaiden.com

Barbara Schutzgruber is an award-winning storyteller of folktales, ballads and personal stories. Since 1987, she has performed over 3,300 programs in schools, prisons, state parks, hospitals, museums, and festivals. She has presented workshops and showcases throughout Michigan, the Midwest, nationally and internationally. She holds a Master's Degree in Children's Literature from Eastern Michigan University. Barbara's website is: http://www.weavestory.com

SYNOPSIS

Beyond the Sword Maiden: A Storyteller's Introduction to the Heroine's Journey is a "how to" book for storytellers, writers, counselors, and anyone who wants to share a story about emotional transformation. We grew up with the hero stories, but found them inadequate and unsatisfying for the events of real life. Stories about injury, illness, divorce, death, and other life struggles are about survivors, not winning heroes.

We searched traditional folktales that dealt with these issues and found a unique storyline—the Heroine's Journey—which is the basis of the book. Readers will find the stories and templates we use to illustrate the steps of the Heroine's Journey easy to follow.

If you have enjoyed this book, consider visiting the following online resources for further reading:

http://www.beyondswordmaiden.com
http://www.weavestory.com

http://www.parkhurstbrothers.com
http://www.storynet.org